YOUNG SKIN

A Literary Horror Novella

BY LINE LANGAGER

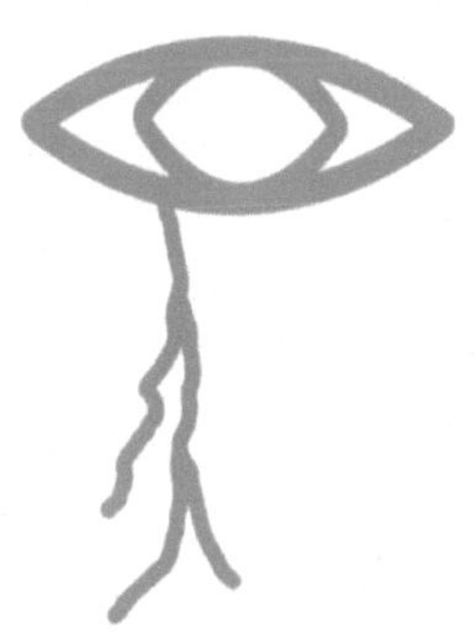

Author: Line Langager

Cover Design: Line Langager (with attributions to freepik.com & vecteezy.com)

Interior Design: Line Langager

ISBN: 978-87-975969-3-7 (paperback)

978-87-975969-4-4 (hardcover)

Publisher: Langager

3. Edition

Dedication

To anyone who can't bear the thought of wasting into the abyss...

Just sign your name here.

____

Contents

Anthem: Radiohead – Climbing Up The Walls

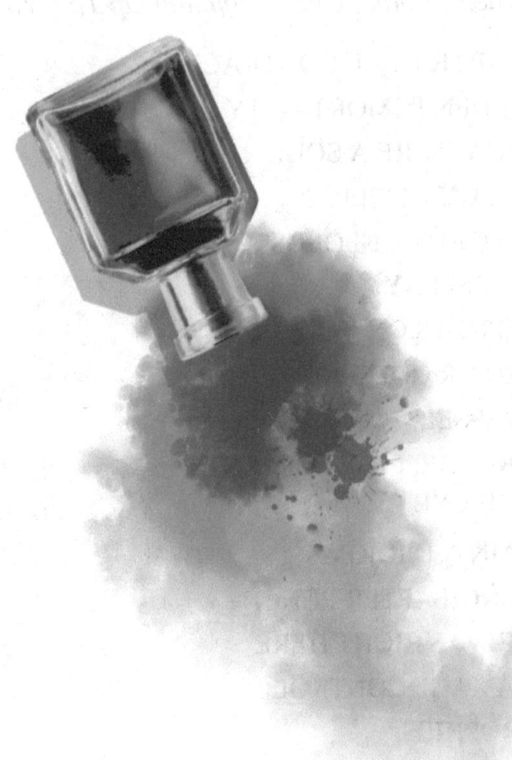

1: A PARTICULAR CONTRACT

The needle buzzes, penetrating the skin. The needle draws blood—and with the blood—little pearls of black ink form on her skin. I can sense my reflection in the mirror as it mimics my every move, the gun vibrating slightly at my command. Every so often, I glance at us. Perhaps to confirm what I already know—that my world is expanding beyond the walls of this studio.

When I wipe at the small of her back, her hands clench into fists by her sides. I finish off for the day by adding the final details to a spectacular solar system in vivid hues of orange and blue. A god's hand extends as though determining the fate of each distant civilisation. Each glistening pearl of ink could be a black hole, as they gape invitingly like voids. The air of the studio tingles with the tang of ink and blood; two inseparable scents.

She stretches her fingers before they tighten back into fists. Her breaths are restrained; every exhalation a deep sigh, mourning the loss of her mortality. I like how it hurts her. Seeing her pain is a reminder of what people are willing to endure to display my art.

The ceaseless buzzing continues in my ear long after I'm done, like a haunting reminder of permanence. An echo of my past, and a window into my future.

I've been sketching and drawing since before I can remember—always carrying a pencil and a piece of paper, often to my mother's dismay when I forgot to empty my pockets before tossing my pants in the laundry.

Perhaps my obsession has been a way to describe emotions, overcome hardships or to express myself. Either way, words have never been my strongest suit. Or rather—not when they have to exit my mouth, at least.

When she notices how I pull back, she tries to get up. I halt her attempt with a raised hand, wondering silently if she understands the depth of the world she has just stepped into—*if she knows that her skin belongs to me*. Her eyes barely skimmed the contract before signing her name.

"Wait," I say, getting to my feet. "I need to photograph you first."

Pulling the camera attached to the ceiling into position, I place myself at my desk while I snap some vivid shots of my latest artwork. It's marvellous—my best work yet. And still, I have this urge to surpass it. That's what keeps me going.

I bring a tube of transparent gel from my supply drawer and apply a thin layer to intensify the colours. I snap a few more shots until I am satisfied.

Click, click.

With my approval, she slowly gets into a seated position on the bench, stretching after several hours of immobility. Her uncovered chest challenges my gaze, but I keep my eyes fixed on hers as they trail around the room, shifting between curiosity and moments of lingering hesitation.

The crimson walls are outlined by white-painted wood panelling, elegantly framing the sparse but chic interior. The walls are covered in anatomical diagrams and paintings in golden frames. Her eyes land on the only piece of displayed artwork in my studio made by me, as though she knows that nothing else compares.

"I can't wait," she says enigmatically, as the stretch of silence snaps.

I pause in my train of thought, derailed by her sudden outburst.

"To become that?" I ask, slightly astonished.

Perched on a pedestal along the wall is a piece of preserved human skin covered in my work—stretched out and encased in a glass frame. Most people would flinch at the sight.

Ever since the young man passed away last month, thereby granting me a static piece of art, the media has been circling me like vultures, closing in.

Controversial business model, they say.

Absurd display of power, they say.

I'm just doing my thing. I tattoo. I display live artwork at my gallery once a month. Everyone who signs a contract with me, must model at my gallery at least once a year. These events attract the necessary attention to keep my business going. To keep my art unique, uninfluenced by my clients.

"No, no—" she says, grimacing slightly, but the expression doesn't linger. "...to see it. I can't wait to see it."

I wish her discomfort wasn't so brief.

"Ahh," I reply, before opening the window to puncture the staleness of the air.

She smirks at me, completely unfazed by the morbid artwork, her chest exposed to the chill September air streaming in. I'm average looking, with unruly dark hair and ink stains on my t-shirt, but women have a tendency to twirl at my feet. Fame gets you anything, really.

Also all the things you don't want.

"Can I see the photos?" she inquires, with her hand tightened around the hem of her blouse.

Her dark hair is tied back into a loose bun at the base of her neck, pulling the attention to her cheekbones as they catch the light.

"Sure."

Pushing back on my desk chair, I allow her to view my screen.

I admire my skillful design, noticing every inch of its perfection, each line and shadow merging seamlessly. I am absorbed in its beauty, forgetting my surroundings when she breaks the silence once more.

"I look good from that angle. Don't you think, Bart? I'm your little masterpiece."

Ignoring her remark, I keep my eyes on the screen, chewing the inside of my cheek.

"I need to cling wrap it before you get dressed. It can't be damaged," I add, getting back on my feet. "You can remove it in a few hours. It heals better if you let it breathe."

The fragile plastic coils slightly, so I trim it before wrapping her entire torso to protect the piece as she returns home. I can't wait for my audience to see this at next month's exhibition. It is the first time I will be displaying the framed skin, too. I cringe slightly at the repercussions, though. The guy's funeral was held only two weeks ago—but I guess it would be sheepish to postpone the inevitable. I just hope the family won't interfere in any way.

Especially legally.

The client wavers in my vicinity, waiting for my eyes to meet her.

They don't.

"You forgot to sign it," she adds, her tone irritating my guts.

“I always sign my work *after* it has healed, at the exhibition. See you next month.”

The repetitiveness of our interactions stirs a heavy sigh, but I hold it in as I toss the gloves and leftover plastics in the bin. When she leaves, so does the air in my lungs.

I lean on the window frame and light a swift cigarette. Cars pass by, some old, some new. My studio is placed on the fourth floor of a bustling street in central Milan. The sound of music is seeping from open windows, impatient car horns are honking. People are chatting loudly on their phones as they cross the street; everything is in motion. Even if you wanted to block it out, it wouldn’t be the same city without it. I watch on in contemplation as my cigarette disappears further between my fingertips with each inhalation, and is, inherently, replaced by another.

Given the impermanence of life, it is human nature to long for preservation of the self. We reproduce to preserve our genes. We photograph every memorable occasion. We write down our deepest thoughts in journals. All in the hope that someone—perhaps simply our future self will consume these preserved moments.

I stub the cigarette. A fragment of a moment of peace, left as a reminder. Something is telling me to hold on to it. Leave it there, sitting in the ashtray.

So I do.

I have a meeting with my manager before next week’s gallery exhibition. My driver honks his horn to grab my attention, but I barely notice him at first as the sound is drowned out by the cacophony of the street below.

He's idling right in front of the entrance to my building, just as I prefer. I close the window and grab my coat, before heading down the stairs.

Outside, the wind gently rustles the trees, shaking loose the leaves of seasons that have passed. The sun's golden rays are reflected on the metallic paint of a bike, casting an eye-catching and iridescent glow. Inside the car, my manager is waiting for me.

2: GOLDEN IMMORTALITY

"*Ciao, ciao*," he says in a friendly tone. His suit is neatly pressed, his hair is combed backwards—a stark contrast to my stained t-shirt.

"So, what's happening today?" I enquire, bypassing pleasantries as the engine whirls to life.

"Oh, you will see that everything will turn out marvellously," he says. "And besides—I have acquired a new... accomplice... with interest in the art world," he adds, with a hint of mystery. "She will bring us what we need. If she decides to show up, that is." I raise my brows in surprise. "She doesn't care about rules or reputations. Just results," he continues, furthering my intrigue.

I like unruly women—less so, when they interfere with my business.

"Is that who we are going to meet today?"

"No. Today I am introducing you to a high-profile client. So wear your best attitude, liven up—don't look so bleak."

"Might've needed a solid 3-5 business days to prepare, in that case." I huff. The car drives across a section of cobblestone, rattling the interior. "Who is your accomplice, then?" I continue, as the scent of my driver's cologne reaches my nostrils.

"She's... intriguing. Difficult—but with a lot of potential," he says, without further explanation.

"And the client?"

"A South African rapper called J-Way. You might've heard of him," he explains. "The guy I've been trying to get in contact with for months. Don't mess this up, he's paying good money."

I do know of J-Way. He's been on the radio frequently. It's rare for me to pay much attention to the lyrics of whatever is playing. I always work in silence at the studio, too. But J-Way has made an impression on me with his flow and unique style. He's been a part of the soundscape of the city for so long, it almost feels climactic to know I'll be meeting him in person.

We pull into the courtyard of a boutique hotel not far from my gallery. The bouncer nods at us as he lets us inside.

The foyer's marble floor elegantly extends into pillars by the curved staircase. We enter the elevator in the company of a guard, who escorts us to a penthouse suite overlooking the heart of the city.

My hands grow clammy the second the door opens. J-Way gets up immediately, his arms splayed to either side in a welcoming gesture.

"Dude, this will be the collab of the century!" he exclaims, shaking my sweaty hand eagerly.

He is dressed in a futuristic white hoodie and matching, loose-fitting pants. His sneakers are chunky, adding to his already towering frame. He seems overly friendly as he gestures for us to sit down—almost larger than life.

My manager adjusts his tie as though the prime minister is present before clearing his throat. The sound makes my toes curl involuntarily, my body stiffening.

"To get the details in place," he says, "I have—I mean, *we* have brought the available designs for you to choose between."

"Yeah," the rapper says. "I sort of get that you don't do customs. To be fair, I wouldn't wanna write a song someone else told me to write."

I nod, appreciating his words. Knowing that my manager has sorted out everything except sketching the actual artworks relaxes me further. I just need to keep my cool.

"Yo, these are neat," he says immediately, his eyes scanning my pristine sketches. It's thrilling to watch him admire them—until he scrunches his face, holding the two sketches on top of each other against the light. "Can you combine these two, though?" he asks, with the late evening sun at his back.

I scrunch my face, not pleased with having to disturb the sceneries I have already perfected. At first, I don't notice it, but when I glance back up at the rapper, it becomes evident that his question wasn't a request.

It was a demand.

My manager pokes at my side without J-Way noticing.

"Possibly," I say stiffly, complying like a dog. "What elements are you interested in?"

He hovers over the polished mahogany coffee table and traces the lines of my abstract imitation of an oil-spill in the ocean. Between clashing waves and sea foam, a human-like goddess rises from the depths covered in hues of oil.

"I like the chaos of this," he says. "But the clouds and the planets are wicked in this one."

"There'd be no balance if we combined them. I drew these separately for a reason," I say dryly.

"Your work speaks. Let's make it louder," he says with a crooked smile, like the decision is already made. "And..." he adds daringly, savouring his final request. "One moment."

Pulling out his phone, he makes a call. Whoever is on the other end of the line picks up immediately, and J-Way begins filling them in.

"*Let's add real gold to it,*" the voice says. "*Just like we talked about.*"

Real gold?

And I thought he wouldn't want to tell me what to do.

"It's my dad," J-Way adds. "He's my manager."

"You want me to embed real gold into... your skin?" I ask, knitting my brows.

"It will look crazy good," he says, confident in his vision. "Dad and I know you can pull off anything."

How would that even work?

My eyes are fixed on J-Way's golden watch as I imagine the artistic ingenuity.

I wish I had thought of that first—if it is possible at all.

But time is ticking.

"If it works, I get the credit for the idea," I begin. "If it doesn't, it was a collaborative experiment."

"Hmm," J-Way and his dad say in unison.

"*Then it's also your job to figure out how to implement it,*" the dad argues. "*Deal?*"

I share a silent look with my manager, who's wearing a tight smile. I can sense him calculating the risks, and yet—he nods.

I hope he knows something I don't.

"Deal," I say.

With the word in free-fall, the air shifts immediately. My manager takes over the financial discussion, albeit struggling slightly to get a word in. The rapper simply leans back in his chair, crossing one leg over the other and lets his father do the talking. The initial price for golden immortality doesn't deter either of them, it seems.

"Just don't forget how much this will benefit you, too," J-Way finally says in a much cooler tone. *More calculated.* "Posting this on my Instagram with your tag will get you mad attention."

"*It will,*" the father adds, his formless voice somehow even more present than the bodyguard.

"We are eternally grateful for your collaboration," my boss says with a hint of pride, but the sweat keeps rubbing off his palms onto his pants.

He is sitting straight up, pants neatly pressed. I barely recognise him during moments like this. His casual flair always dissolves as soon as we step out of the car.

J-Way sucks his teeth for a moment. The bodyguard shifts his weight. I can feel his eyes scrutinizing us, observing our every move, forcing me to behave like a puppet on strings.

On the other side of the panoramic window, the skyline of Milan is carved into the horizon while an airplane drags a white line across the cloudless sky. As my manager uneasily checks his wristwatch, I realise just how fragile this deal is.

What goes up must come back down.

"Don't forget that Bart is posting your photos too," my manager says stiffly.

Heels click faintly as light footsteps approach the door. Everyone turns their attention to the entrance and someone knocks gently. We all fall silent.

The bodyguard swiftly opens the sleek wooden door, exchanging a few low murmurs with a woman.

Although I only get a glimpse of her before looking at J-Way again, she's obviously stunning.

"I have to go," J-Way says apologetically. "Promised my girl a dinner date before my show tonight."

My manager is visibly sweaty now. Without a signed document, it's worthless.

"And the contract?" he asks, an unfamiliar uncertainty causing his voice to tremble ever so slightly.

"Just make me the combined sketch and get the golden ink, and I'll go with your €38k," he says. "See you on Monday for the first session."

Without further discussion, he is out of the door. My manager lets out a prolonged sigh of relief, deflating into his usual slouch. The bodyguard gestures for us to leave the room, his broad figure looming above us. I can feel him breathe down my neck as he leads us all the way down the hallway, down the elevator and out through the overly extravagant lobby. As we step onto the bustling sidewalk, paparazzi start flashing their cameras.

"Did you sign a contract agreement with the rapper J-Way?" one asks in a piercing voice.

"What does it feel like to be the most controversial artist of the decade?" another tries, her microphone propped on a stick, poking it in my direction.

I ignore their remarks with a straight face. My driver opens the door to the backseat, and I slide in. The car sets into motion before the door shuts out the cacophony of the streets around us. As I buckle my seatbelt, though, we have already escaped the chaos by detouring slightly. Before returning to my street, my driver pulls into a gas station and leaves us for a few minutes to talk. He doesn't pump the gas. He just walks straight into the small shop.

For a moment the neon sign above the shop's sliding door flashes, before settling in a dim, red colour. My manager is breathing through his mouth as he types rapidly on his phone.

I hate when he does that.

I break the silence as my mind keeps whirling around the same question.

"Where are we going to get golden ink from?" I ask.

"Money can buy you anything," he says in a whisper, despite the driver being gone. "I will get that sorted."

"I need to see it before I beli—"

"...you are incurably pessimistic, Bart. Nothing good will come of it. Nothing good, if you don't let it. It's like not cooking the pasta at all just because you are scared it will be overcooked. I will serve you what you ordered."

I roll my eyes at him.

"Sure," I say, mostly to end his rant before it derails completely.

"You will hear from my accomplice when she's ready for you," my manager says, a little more restrained, as the driver returns empty-handed and places the electric key on the pad to start the car again. Instead of returning to the studio, he pulls up by my local bar. *He knows me better than most.* "—or so I hope," he continues, his voice returning to a sort of forced whisper.

I simply nod as we part ways. There's nothing left to be said once he has made up his mind. Instead, I watch the black BMW glide elegantly down the lane and disappear behind a corner before I slip into the bar.

3: TO CAPTURE A SOUL

My usual spot is empty.

I light a long awaited cigarette, easing into the evening. With the warm air of the bar gently embracing me, I rest the cigarette on the tray in front of me and take off my jacket. Folding it over my lap, my lighter tumbles to the sticky, tiled floor. I shrug. The TV hums with the commentary of an unimportant soccer game. I glance at it distractedly, my mind wandering.

Who is this new, unpredictable accomplice?

The smoke from my cigarette mingles with the stale, sour smell of spilled beer. I ask for a pint, knowing I'm off for the weekend. The bartender nods as she pours me a glass to the sound of the tap's pump, the foam soon trembling at the brim.

The thought of embedding gold into skin makes my hands tingle with anticipation. There's something alchemical about the idea. It's grand. Gold has been used for centuries to crown kings and adorn the elite. Now, it will be encapsulated in the flesh of a modern rapper—uprooting the laws of power and ethics.

“Hungry?” the bartender disrupts my train of thought, well aware this is the only place I ever eat.

“The usual,” I reply, a creature of inherited habit.

My dad used to frequent this place when I was a kid. It’s nostalgic with its dark wooden panels and beige tiles. During the day, it’s a cafe. I tend to swing by for a coffee and a croissant, although I never cared much for food—but it turns out to be essential.

“How is the new deal going for you?” the bartender asks, sparking conversation. “The tabloids are on you like hawks,” she adds with a hint of a laugh.

“It’s a work in progress,” I admit. “The legal issues... the parents of the client who passed away are trying to sue me. I’m trying to keep up.”

The sound of laughter from another table is muffled by the music from the speakers.

“It’s a bold move,” she says. “When will you be showing off the framed... *you know*... for the first time?’

“On Wednesday,” I say. “You should come.”

She grimaces theatrically.

“I’m not sure I have the guts for that.”

She laughs, but her expression quickly changes.

An elderly man stumbles past me, mumbling about the lack of moral development the youth exudes these days.

"You, young man, should take a very long look at your peculiar ambitions," he lectures. "One day it will all come cascading down the drain. Don't tell me I didn't warn you!"

He shakes a tabloid in my face, mumbling between hiccups. I catch a glimpse of my rugged face bathed in flashing lights, my hollow eyes betraying my disgust for the media.

I hate relying on them for exposure.

The headline reads:

'A contract with the devil: Would you sign up for immortality?'

Before heading out of the bar, the man stumbles into a chair, cursing its existence. I attempt to share a look of annoyance with the bartender, but she simply laughs as I roll my eyes. Perhaps it's an omen—but the thought of vanishing into obscurity terrifies me more than the cost of my ambition.

My bolognese slowly disappears from the plate while I maintain a distant glare at the relic of a TV. It's always displaying the sports channel and the spaghetti sauce isn't evenly heated. At least those things are reliable.

With mechanical movements, I signal for another pint. Its condensation is cool against my fingertips as I nurse it, and I drag out the time between each sip to savour the peace.

When I'm done, I toss a handful of coins on the bar without counting.

As I leave, the night greets me with a gush of chill air. I cross the street haphazardly, manoeuvring the late evening traffic. Someone yells at me to get out of their way. The usual. All except the moon. It hangs low, casting hues of ominous red on my path.

...

In between sketchbooks and stubbed pencils, old mugs of coffee and yellow sticky notes, I reconstruct the sketch for J-Way. The goddess rises from the depths of chaos, her form both divine and corrupted, gold threading through the lines of her silhouette. I bring the clouds from my other sketch, twirling them around her figure. It is chaotic. *Senseless*. Just what he asked for.

I'm putting the final touches on the golden moon when my phone rings. It's my manager. At first, I let it ring. There's something particularly satisfying about making him wait.

His sharp voice cuts directly to business. I don't mind that.

"*An elderly woman has approached me*," he says immediately. "*She wants to be immortalized before it is too late. A potential candidate for your contract agreement. She's an old model. Just excellent*."

I scratch my head with the back of my pencil. The eraser falls off the end, and I feel the sharp metal dig into my scalp briefly.

"When is she coming to see me?" I inquire, rubbing the sore spot on my head.

"*If you can make time for her today, it would be great,*" he says.

"And the gold?" I ask. "I haven't figured out how to safely embed it yet. There isn't any available information online."

"*Gold dust,*" my manager says with confidence. "*I'm trying to obtain the finest product for you to mix with your ink. 24 carats. I will get back to you soon. Can you fit in Vera, the old model, today?*"

I cast a glance around my studio. I have nothing else to do, so I agree.

"Sure," I reply, already digging through my sketchbooks to see if anything could be used immediately. "I'll handle it."

He hangs up.

Thirty minutes later, a faint, distinct knock echoes through the studio. I scurry to the door, smoothing out the wrinkles on my shirt. The face I meet on the other side is poised, with an elegance carved by time, yet lit by an undeniable energy.

“Ah,” Vera says, her eyes expanding playfully. “My key to eternal life.”

A tight smile forms on my lips. I gesture for her to enter the studio, mirroring her regal posture. She moves with the ease of someone accustomed to admiration, her eyes trailing along the interior.

“You know, I always liked how much the ancient Egyptians honoured the dead,” she says, studying the displayed piece of skin.

The case is brightly lit, allowing every detail to be illuminated.

“To not be remembered, is to never have existed,” I muse, searching her sparkling eyes for approval. “Right?”

“Indeed.”

She nods, her sleek hair and dark, prominent eyes still striking despite her years.

“Do you have any particular designs in mind?” I ask. “—or would you perhaps... allow me to experiment?”

I wasn’t quite able to put together something prior to seeing her. It’s like the artwork has to merge with the person, otherwise it doesn’t work. I didn’t fully comprehend the extent of what my teacher told me in art school when he said that my drawings lacked soul—until I started tattooing. For a few months after that comment, I stopped drawing entirely. Then I slowly started to sketch people. Then gods.

"I would never tell a painter what to paint," she says with the ghost of a smile. "Neither will I hinder your creativity."

"Great," I reply, relieved to have a moment to unfold my mind. "Let me free-hand a sketch on your back so it suits your every detail. Working with your beauty marks, rather than against them," I say.

I raise the black leather bench into a suitable position for her. She undresses as needed and leans forwards on its cool, sterilized surface.

"You used to model?" I ask sincerely.

"Oh yes, for fifty years," she says, her voice full of pride.

I have never worked on loose skin before. It's a challenge to bring the image to life, but with one, purposeful line at a time, a goddess takes shape from a bed of multi-coloured wildflowers. Young skin is like a living canvas—this is a canvas that has already lived.

"What was it like," I ask. "Modelling?"

She seems to ponder briefly.

"Oh I have so many stories to tell," she says, slightly muffled by the bench. "I have travelled the world. Fallen in love..." she trails off. "What have you procured for me?" she asks, her voice filled with intrigue.

I allow her to view my hand-drawn sketch in the mirror. Her head tilts slightly, as she determines its fate.

"It is as though you captured my spirit in this," she says. "Let's go ahead."

...

As the first session with Vera draws to a close, we shake hands. Dusk is setting in, weaving its gloomy light through the thin curtains.

"We should go for a coffee sometime," she says. "Your work fascinates me."

"I would be honoured," I reply, as I hold the door for her.

The floor right outside of the door is visibly worn, the wood softly dented by decades of shuffling feet.

"Your art preserves us," she says, her voice almost reverent. "It feels like cheating death."

I nod a single time, and she tucks in her chin in response.

As she leaves, her silhouette seems to retract into the darkness of the hallway, like part of her soul has been allowed to let go.

"*She wants to be immortalized before it is too late*," my boss had said.

I wonder how long she has left.

I wonder what happens to souls that will never be laid to rest.

I stay the night in the backroom like I do most nights. I prefer it here. My apartment is dull, and its blandness strips away my creativity like turpentine to paint. The walls here are adorned with artists I admire, as well as a pinned sketch or two—abandoned concepts of past inspirations. The atmosphere is undeniable. It feels lived in.

As I sink into my mattress, vivid images of dreamlike quality immediately begin filling my mind.

I drift off to sleep.

4: THE ACCOMPLICE

In the morning, I drop by the cafe as usual. People chatter and glasses clink behind the counter as the day begins to take shape. The scent of freshly baked bread is inviting, and the whir of the coffee grinder periodically muffles the chatter from the tables. The sound is soothing, dulling the soundscape of a world I only experience in glimpses.

When I step back outside with my croissant in one hand and a coffee in the other, a woman stumbles into me, blocking my way. She regains her footing quickly, adjusting her casual office wear.

"Aren't you on your way to work or something?' I hiss, my voice laced with exasperation.

She huffs at me, her features narrowing beneath a pair of huge sunglasses.

"I am never on my way to work—work is always on its way to me."

I frown at her as she unlocks her car from a distance with a deliberate gesture. The beep echoes through the street, startling a fat pigeon. Her black hair reflects the pale sunlight, ignited by her act of rebellion amidst the chaos of the street.

"Get in," she demands, her heels already clicking against the pavement, her back turned to me.

What?

I stare at her for a moment, as she enters the car and shuts the door behind her in one motion. A moment of passivity passes before she rolls down the window and makes a frustrated *come-on* movement with her left hand. Irritated, I turn 90 degrees on my heel, aiming to cross the street to my studio—but an unknown man in dark shades walks uncomfortably close to me, pausing briefly in his step.

"You don't want to do that," he says matter-of-factly, placing a hand on my bicep, guiding me back on the sidewalk.

Despite my confusion, I comply.

In silence, we drive across the city centre and out through the heavy traffic into Monza. Towering buildings and industrial zones give way to narrower streets.

At every red light, her finger begins tapping restlessly on the steering wheel. The interior is jet-black.

I wonder if her intentions are dark, too.

Lush greenery sprinkles the landscape in hues of Autumn, creating a powerful juxtaposition with the concrete blocks in the rearview mirror.

I only realise how I keep holding my breath once I let out a forced gasp. I cast a quick glance at her. She doesn't react. There's something quite striking about her profile, the tip of her nose curved slightly upwards.

I clench my hands around my paper cup. My coffee has gone cold. The drive seems to go on forever, pulling me further and further away from the life I know.

She rolls down the window and places a slim cigarette between her lips. Instead of lighting it herself she waves her hand at me.

"Will you?"

Keeping her eyes on the road, she waits for me to obey.

I fumble for the lighter in my pocket. As it flickers to life, the scent of lighter fluid momentarily tinges the air, before it is swept away by the cool current.

The lane curves elegantly, extending through a valley. Between clutches of trees, I get a glimpse of the breathtaking view. If I had brought a sketchbook, I'd not have hesitated to memorialize this moment. The lake reflects the clouds above as they are carried by the wind. We must be north of Monza now.

The woman inhales deeply and blows out the smoke through the side of the outlined lips. The tires barely grip the asphalt on the steep road as she begins to slow down at last.

We pull into a street that clings to the mountainside. The sound of the doors unlocking seems exaggerated as they echo in the valley below, and birdsong replaces the silence between us. She looks at me straight on for the first time, her expression unreadable.

"Look what the cat dragged in," she says, her sarcasm ringing through the air, before taking a final drag on the cigarette and tossing it on the stone path.

She steps on it with precision before guiding me through the entrance, and I follow her through the house. Each shadow we pass seems more oppressing than the last, the walls tightening their grip on me.

"Please sit down," she says. "Wait here. And for the love of God, please drink your coffee."

I reluctantly bring the cup to my lips, my hand trembling slightly as I gulp the entire thing in one go, my dry throat thankful for the bitter liquid. She nods once, seemingly pleased, before leaving the room.

A click swiftly follows—*she just locked me in.*

I listen to her footsteps while they fade further into the house, as though swallowed by a void. Still clenching my cup, I stare at the peeling paint near the door handle as the sound of my own breath begins to disturb me. Lungs filling. Air exiting. I exist in a vacuum. I have the strange sensation of a presence. Nothing stirs. And yet—everything does.

Am I truly alone?

By the time she returns, my fingers have gone stiff from the cold.

She raises her eyebrows, placing a stack of seemingly fresh laundry on the chair opposite me. Her sunglasses are now in her hair, revealing a pair of dark brown eyes lined with charcoal.

"Uhh," I sort of say, but she interrupts me.

"...well, since that is out of the way. Let's talk."

"Is this an interrogation?" I ask with genuine wonder.

She looks at me in confusion, staring at me blankly as though I were a cashier at a supermarket unable to scan her pack of smokes. Her foot is tapping restlessly on the stone floor.

"Didn't your boss tell you I was coming?"

"Well, sort of," I admit.

But this is not exactly what I had expected.

"Great," she says, as though this resolved everything. "Regarding your... business model," she begins.

"Yeah?"

"Although intriguing, it is... flawed."

I scrunch my face, scratching my stubbled chin.

"How so?"

"You see—people don't just *die*. You are going to outlive your clients," she explains, pacing back and forth in the office. "Or at least you will if you quit smoking like a chimney."

"What do you propose?" I enquire, ignoring her comment. The detergent on the laundry permeates the air, a fragrance of normality. *Of life*. "It's not like we can just make people—"

"...die young?" she adds, sending shivers down my spine.

"I showcase my art on living canvases already."

I attempt to amend the direction of the conversation, pursuing the lesser evil.

She shakes her head slowly. The bookcase behind her is visibly dusty.

"But you noticed how much attention the news of the preserved piece got you, right? And it hasn't even been displayed yet."

"Sure," I reply, remembering how people queued down the sidewalk at my most recent exhibition, asking for autographs and photos.

"And I bet that felt good, right?"

She is smirking now.

Although my head is nodding in acknowledgement, I grab the armrest of the chair a bit tighter.

Where's she going with this?

"Let's double it," she adds, with a daring look in her eyes. My manager's words echo in my head: *She doesn't care about rules or reputation—just results.* When I don't reply, she decides to continue. "Bart?"

My finger is digging into the fabric of the armrest, as the sound of her foot tapping impatiently on the floor resumes.

My art teacher is still alive, and frankly, people have a tendency to become numb to the obscure if it doesn't keep evolving. I want him to see what art truly is. What *my* art can do.

I hesitate, choosing my words carefully.

"If you can make sure art teacher Mr. Dal Lago will attend every single exhibition I ever have, and that every exhibition will outperform the last—" I begin. "Then do it. I don't care how."

"I can make anything happen," she says, her words lingering in the air. "As long as you are willing to pay."

5: A LEGACY UNFOLDS

The drive back feels like pulling the day in reverse. The same view, the same oppressive silence—just backwards. As we near Milan, I am struck by a twinge of homesickness, watching the city from the periphery. I never leave Milan. In fact, I realise now that this has been the first time since I was a kid.

When she drops me off at my local bar in the evening, I realise why everything ties back to this bar. Why I keep returning like the tide, only to push away everyone before I retract.

My dad left nothing behind but a shadow. Since his passing, no one has mentioned his name. It is like he never existed at all—except he created me. Despite everything, it taught me one lesson; if we want to be remembered, we have to force the world to see us. When I think about my dad, the hazy outline is barely a sketch. A faceless being, devoid of expressions. A silhouette of someone who could've been anyone.

A glass slips from the bartender's hands, clattering into the sink of dishes. I can feel it in my teeth.

It's the same girl who is tending the bar tonight. She slides me a beer without any questions.

"This one is on the house," she says, drying off a glass with a dirty rag. "Looks like you've had a day."

My stale croissant is chewy and dry, and the flakes fall down my shirt. I don't bother brushing them off. The bartender studies me—I don't have to look in her direction to feel her eyes on me. It doesn't exactly feel like pity. Not that I'd need that, anyway.

The crumbs still cling to my shirt as I get up, emptying the glass of the last swig of beer.

I return to my studio. Tomorrow morning, J-Way will be here for his first session. I hope my manager has resolved the issue with the gold. If not, I will implement it later. The low hum of cars passing through the street lulls me to sleep before I can form any further thoughts.

Thankfully.

The backroom has no windows, so when the doorbell buzzes at 8am, I emerge from my chamber like a dishevelled bear out of hibernation. I pull on the nearest shirt I can get hold of before opening the door.

J-Way greets me with his infamous crooked smile, his diamond-embellished tooth glinting in the harsh light of the studio. His bodyguard sends me a silent warning; *don't mess this up*. I nod a single time.

A miserable attempt at masking my fatigue.

As they both enter, their eyes are immediately caught by the glass vitrine. The bodyguard's judgemental stare lingers on the encased piece of skin—a vicious critique of my obscure monument.

I stifle a yawn.

I wish I'd had at least a cigarette. But J-Way isn't the kind of customer you keep waiting, so we get straight to work. He has booked me for the entire day to stay within his time limit before heading back to South Africa. I believe two full days will be sufficient, but we need to allow a few weeks of healing before the next session.

I wipe down the bench. The antiseptic tinges the air briefly before it evaporates. Its existence is so fragile, yet so impactful while it lasts.

The sketch is neatly printed onto the hectograph. I place the stencil and press it onto his warm back. My tattoo machine reflects the light, gleaming.

"This is looking good, man," J-Way says, content with my sketch. "Exactly what I had in mind." I do a double check before the first ink meets his skin. "Oh-ho-ho, how I missed that sound. The pain is just a bonus."

"How's the tour going, anyway?" I ask, having a go at a regular human interaction.

"The crowd is so different here," he says. "More restrained. I could barely get a mosh-pit going, but they figured it out when my hit single started blasting."

"Where are you going next?" I ask as the outline of the goddess begins to take shape.

"France, then Germany," he explains, completely unfazed by the searing pain. "Then I'll be back here for your next session."

"Great," I say.

I feel powerful knowing a famous musician has adapted his tour plan just to make time for me.

He allows me to work in relative peace until our lunch break. We order some sushi and I finally get a chance to smoke. He bites his cheek as he twists his neck to see how far we've come.

In a kind of silence that feels like a presence, he purses his lips and flicks his gaze towards me in the mirror.

"Where's the gold?" he asks in a much cooler tone.

It spreads like a frostbite in the air, twisting unease into my chest. I swallow hard. A grain of sticky rice is still stuck in my throat.

"I— I have to finish the outline first," I explain. "To uhmm... know where to place it."

"But you got it, right?" his tone is deep and dominant now—it's almost a growl.

"My manager does," I say to the wide-jawed lion in front of me, without knowing whether it's true.

I refuse to let anyone ruin my success with their incompetence. My own turmoil is causing enough trouble already.

How will I get it, if he can't?

He gets back in position, gesturing for me to resume my work. I close the window, and attempt to block out the tension in the air. It could create steam as it pulsates like the buzzing needle.

One wrong move can ruin my reputation.

I pull back, letting go of a heavy breath.

J-Way chuckles as though our last interaction was a figment of my imagination.

"Tough work?"

"You wouldn't even know," I reply drily, diving back into the depths of the swirling sea that splashes against the goddess on his skin.

I don't glance at the clock until the final stroke of black ink has come to life. I don't have to, to know it's late. It's already dark outside.

The bodyguard repeats his gesture of silent warning as J-Way takes a look at the result. I stretch my aching fingers, and pride rushes through me when both men nod their approval. Pride *and* relief.

We shake hands, and I slip the bodyguard a note with the details of our next appointment.

I've got loose threads to tie.

...

I'm on the phone with my manager the entire evening while I browse the web looking for answers. As it turns out, he *hasn't* figured out *shit*. His kids are loud in the background and our conversation is fragmented.

"Gold has a melting point of over a thousand degrees," I say in exasperation.

"*Hold on for a moment*," he says, putting me on hold. I sigh, pulling at my hair with one hand while the other continues scrolling. My finger is stiff by now, the movement unnervingly mechanical. The line scrambles back to life. "*Here's the solution*," my manager says at last. "*Transparent ink, fine gold dust and a slightly larger needle.*"

"We will need to test this," I say. The full moon casts a pale, iridescent glow across my desk, partially disturbed by the transparent curtains. I lean my elbow on the desk, dreary with exhaustion. "When can you get me these items?"

"*By next week*," he replies without hesitation. "*How did the meeting with Rosaline go anyway? I didn't have the time to ask her.*"

"You mean the kidnapping?" I joke, but I tense at the words, realizing that she never even introduced herself.

"Oh, don't be so sly; she just handles things in her own way," he says, his son interrupting him once more. A shrill scream echoes through the receiver, and I drop my phone on my desk. The muffled chaos continues on his end, a disruption of our calculated efforts to plan. I flare my nostrils and my jaw tightens. "*...I'll have to get these monkeys caged for the night, see you on Wednesday.*"

I can hear his son giggle at the word monkey before the line is cut off.

I grit my teeth, vexed by his chaotic home life and willingness to compromise. I cast a glance at the stacks of sketches on my cluttered desk—a result of relentless attention to detail, each representing a layer of improved talent. My ascent into stardom. This is what I built my name on; careful planning and one precise line at a time. Suddenly depending on a reckless deal could jeopardize my entire career.

The evening turns to night as I continue to scroll through forums discussing similar theories. Not a single person has managed this before.

But I'll have to.

I take a quick shower before stepping onto the bath mat. My hollow eyes stare back at me, unimpressed—the ghost of my father.

Is he proud of me?

Have I gone far enough to uproot the generational curse of eventual evaporation?

I tousle my hair with the towel and get into bed. I need to get a grip.

...

Tuesday comes and goes. I don't leave the studio until I absolutely have to.

The bar is empty except for the local drunk. He is slumped on a bench in the corner below the TV.

"Tomorrow's the big day," the bartender says as I take a seat. She's wiping the counter, probably just to keep her hands busy. "How are you feeling?"

I can hear the drunk guy snoring.

"I'd like for you to come," I say, surprising even myself.

She appears to consider my request, her lips pursed in contemplation.

"I'll be there," she says with a smile. I never noticed her dimple before. "Anything for my favourite customer."

Satisfied with her reply, I order a piece of lasagna to get myself out of my groove. The steam rises, swirling in the air from the fan, giving way to new patterns.

"You're experimenting today," she says in a delighted tone. "What's the occasion?"

"I always search for new inspiration in the mundane," I say, imagining how God created man from nothing as he gazed upon the empty world.

"Mundane," she laughs. "I'd never have guessed that lasagna and death would go hand in hand."

I huff, my chest rising in an unfamiliar movement.

"Do you ever feel... guilty?" she asks, her voice low and filled with buried questions.

The snoring patron snaps for breath. For a few snores, I swallow the frustration that seems to build in my throat.

Why would I?

Should I?

"I don't see why I should," I say stiffly. "I simply offer a service. A deal of mutual interest. It's not like people are forced to choose me as their artist."

She tilts her head. The half-empty liquor bottles gleam in the flickering light. She studies my face. Not in a judgemental way, but out of curiosity.

She looks at me like I have become one with my art—*and perhaps she is right.*

6: ON DISPLAY

I arrive early for the exhibition to coordinate with the staff and my models. A white, multi-levelled platform is displaying the models, while my framed piece will be sectioned off in a dark room. The case will be illuminated brightly, with the oppressive darkness enhancing the experience.

The press is at the entrance, huddled together in a desperate formation. I allow myself to smile for the cameras as I gesture for the first group of visitors to enter. People are queueing down the sidewalk and around the corner. I watch as they are herded like sheep by the exhibition guards, and a buzzing warmth wells up in my torso.

My manager is going to love this.

"Are you obsessed with legacy?" one journalist asks as I let her inside.

"I'd rather let you decide for yourself," I reply, my narrow mouth growing wider.

A sign with the words '*no photos allowed*' is printed in red, adding suspense to the entrance. The public has only read a description of the exhibition and its newest addition—nothing quite beats the first impressions.

I shake a bunch of hands on my way through the gallery. The naked, white floor and walls force the attention onto the art. Mixed reactions bounce off each other, allowing for philosophical debates. People chatter in respectful, low murmurs. I like the prestige of museums—the way people engage with the art as though it were sentient.

And well, here it is.

Twelve models stand like living monuments, only their breaths and occasional blinking betraying their connection to life.

Perhaps that is all life is. *Breathing. Blinking.* Until the day it stops.

I step into the dark chamber. Like a tomb, it exudes an eerie presence. *Immortality*—it truly exists. For effect, I have added large speakers in each corner that pulsate with the sound of a beating heart. The allure is undeniable.

As I observe the visitors, I begin to gauge the vastness of my power. People gasp when they enter the darkness, absorbed by its contents. I see what Rosaline meant; I *do* want more.

Despite this, I wander the space, searching every face I pass, to know if she kept her promise. The first hour passes without a sight of Mr. Del Vago. Then the next.

All except a pair of curators fall silent when I walk into the chamber. The men continue talking, but their features are hidden in the dark.

"I thought there'd be more by now," one says, gesturing at the case.

"There are. I bet he's just holding them back for the sake of charging extra next month."

My fist clenches, but when I get a glimpse of the bartender, I release the tension. Seeing her out of her usual environment, wearing her own clothes—she seems so out of place and vulnerable. An intrusion in my world.

She approaches me, shielding her eyes from the exhibition, over-exaggerating her disgust for the macabre display.

"It is so much worse in real life," she says, but her playful gesture fades as her gaze returns to the mummified remains. "I didn't think it would feel... so human. So real."

"Thank you for coming, anyway," I say, genuinely pleased, although something seems to change in the air between us.

We stand for a while, observing side by side, before she turns to face me again. She tilts her head slightly, parting her lips as though to say something—but loud voices from the front exhibition catch our attention. Our eyes flick towards the sound in synchrony before meeting again in the low light.

"That doesn't sound good," she whispers.

Scrunching my face, I leave her behind in the dark with a look of apology.

Scanning the room, I find my manager frantically discussing with an old couple. Their backs are facing me, but their upset is unmistakably twisted into every gesticulation.

"What is going on?" I demand at the top of my lungs, yearning to resolve the dispute before it disrupts my visitors.

As people step aside to let me view the scene in full, and I see my manager's face drained of confidence, I begin shaking my head slowly.

Whatever this is, it isn't good.

"The artwork belongs to Ra—" he clears his throat. "To Bart Giovanni!"

I raise a hand to signal for the arguing to stop, taking a deep breath to avoid returning the tone of frustration. It takes me a moment to recognize their faces. But when I do, I grow a lump in my throat.

It's the parents of the deceased.

...

The mother is clinging desperately to her husband's arm, as though to cling to life itself. Her lips tremble as she points towards thc tomb of their fragmented son.

Then straight at me.

"You!" her voice sharp like a blade's edge, piercing through the murmuring crowd. Her finger remains hovering with accusation and everyone falls silent. "You did this to our son!"

I bite my lip as all eyes fall on me. The bartender's question replays in my head. *Guilt?* That's not a feeling I associate myself with.

I hesitate briefly, waiting for the crowd to stop murmuring.

"He signed a contract," I reply matter-of-factly.

...and he did, although he never even glanced at the details. I also didn't stab him. Or steal his car. But *someone* did.

Clenching his fists by his sides, the father's jaw tightens until an angry vein protrudes from his forehead.

"He did *not* know what he signed up for!" he exclaims, his voice hoarse with regret, as though his words could amend his failure to protect his son.

I roll my eyes. The guy was around my age. A grown man makes his own decisions—*and his own mistakes, too*, I think.

Hushed voices of concern from the crowd send a wave of goosebumps across my skin.

"A bit late for that," someone adds, directed at the father.

Faces turn towards the voice shrouded by the crowd. When I search for the intruder, I see him at last—Mr. Del Vago is standing front and centre, worn by a decade of scrutiny. His features have drooped further, leaving a permanent expression of distaste. He looks at me like I have failed him again.

I will not allow that.

The mother's eyes flicker between me and the bold stranger. Her breath catches as she clings tighter to her husband.

"We demand to get back his remains," the father continues, his voice ringing through the gallery as though it were empty.

The disturbance makes the room feel sterile, like he just stripped away the magic of art, leaving behind a shell. I want to crunch something in my fist. The bones in my hand could snap at the force.

Nobody is stealing the soul of my art.

"Go somewhere else to mourn," I say in a flat tone. "The exit is right there."

I gesture for the guard to escort them out of the gallery while avoiding the eyes of the world. To my surprise, though, the father strides directly past me and into the chamber, the guard and the mother right at his tail. As the father howls with sorrow and clammers onto the frame, his grubby hands leave fingerprints all over the glass. As he wails, the guard attempts to unhinge him from the art, but as he does so, the frame begins to wobble. My manager shouts through the exhibition for a second guard to intervene, and I rush to steady the artwork as the two guards pull off the intruder with force.

Gasps spread like a wildfire as people stiffen in their spot. A whole room full of living dolls, a brief but unnerving sight. The grimy fingerprints disturb the case, creating a layer of desperation I can't unsee.

Shortly after the parents have been removed, a conservator examines the frame for possible damage. As he cleans the surface, people slowly continue moving about the exhibition, feeding the kind of infamy I've built my name on.

Art prospers beneath a flame.

It ignites.

And this is just the beginning.

7: IT GROWS ON YOU

The media backlash that follows the incident is captivating. They call me deviant; questioning both my craft and my personal motivations. My Instagram is filled with accusations, but also with respect. People are awestruck. *I need them to be split.* There's power in heated discussions—they spill through the gaps of society, *widening them*, until everyone knows my name. Until everyone's thumbs are typing out my name on search engines, spreading my concept like a contagious plague.

A few of my models have been accused of being complicit as the scandal began to spill over. Several were asked if they were bribed into submission. None of them were, and so they stated. Yet, the words '*moral disturbance of society*' continue stirring up dust.

Let them.

My manager calls me the following day to meet him on the sidewalk. I grab the collar of my coat and pull it on as I run down the stairs. Each step creaks in its own tune, like an old piano worn by time.

When the car door closes behind me, Rosaline pulls out into the heavy traffic. My manager is seated in the back, hands resting on his knees like a school kid.

“Told you,” she says as though continuing an ongoing conversation. “The infamy grows on you.” I scratch the back of my head, the purr of the diesel engine a steady backdrop. “Like I said, I can make anything happen.”

Her eyes remain fixed on the lane ahead, even though the car is barely in motion. It feels like we’ve been vacuum sealed.

Maybe we *are* contagious.

“Consider this,” my manager begins, shifting in his seat. “In its current state, the gold-embedded tattoo is just a hypothesis to the public. It will remain so until the day people get to see it.”

“Now imagine how much attention it would draw if it was in your possession,” Rosaline adds. “How many visitors. How many followers online.”

“Where are you going with this?” My intrigue is piqued despite my growing discomfort. The two emotions wrestle, tying impossible knots in my chest. “And it isn’t exactly more than a hypothesis to me, either,” I continue. “Did you even *get* the gold?”

She purses her lips briefly before replying, waving a hand as she speaks.

"Yes, yes. We have it. Either way, I'm *suggesting—*" she says, emphasising the word, letting it linger. "—I propose a calculated setup, building slowly but steadily... to get you what you need to enhance your profile in the art world. To keep you one step ahead of anyone else."

I blink, barely daring to ask. My lips part to ask the question: *How?* But my tongue goes numb, tingling against the roof of my mouth.

I know *what* I need. At this point, I just don't know who told me I need it.

Ahead, yes, someone whispers to me from my periphery, as the car idles in the heavy traffic. I flick my head in the direction of the sound, but I already feel myself nodding as though invisible strings were pulling at my head. My parched soul is drenched in her promise. I forget my morality. I keep nodding. The appeal is too nourishing. I want *more*. I want people to know my name and not just say it. I need their voices laced with timorousness and respect.

I catch my manager's eye in the rear-view mirror. Sweat glistens on his forehead, nostrils flared.

"Like your exhibition taught us," Rosaline continues, unfazed by his discomfort. "Nothing quite stirs attention like *loss*."

My manager smiles, but it stiffens into a grimace, like his portrait was painted onto the mirror.

Some remnant of me recoils as she pulls down a narrow street, its lane cast in ominous shadows. I swallow hard, even though I have nothing to swallow. My head fills with overlapping voices, none of which is my own.

They whisper.

They whisper.

Such strange words.

Perhaps if I listened, I would hear a warning—*but I don't.* Instead, I feel the pull of the underworld, covering my ears like a kid, as the cul-de-sac narrows ahead.

...

In a haze, I am dropped off somewhere familiar. Heavy drops of rain pelt against the pavement, tinging the air with the scent of wet asphalt. The hedge is overgrown, and the steel trellis of dead, brownish roses rustles against the façade. *It's really been that long*, I think, as my gaze travels the trellis, only to find another perished plant on the windowsill of my apartment.

Why did she drop me off here?

I shrug, sticking my hand in my pocket to dig out my keys. When I traverse the steps to the front door, though, it feels more like I'm intruding than returning home. No one is here to greet me.

The name on the door next to mine has been changed. An empty cardboard box is sitting in a vacant corner, marking an end and a new beginning, all at the same time.

The hallway feels tight with absence, making me shrink to fit the confines of what could've been my home. A home is built, nurtured. This is a mocking shell of convenience.

Despite my suffocation, I spend the evening digging through old sketchbooks. Going through them in chronological order somehow soothes my mind, as I watch myself improve with every stroke. Focusing on something so intently has always been a refuge for me. It only makes sense to keep going. Every last page of every sketchbook is a new reason to expand my vision. *And I do.* Larger pages, more details. More ink. More soul. Page after page, I build courage.

Courage to do what has to be done.

8: MAN OR GOD

I wake to a phone call from Vera. It's been a hectic week of damage control after the scrutinising tabloids tried to shred my business model. The majority of the time, I've been hiding in my apartment, dealing with the aftermath through my manager. I'll let him sort it out. That'll ensure that the press misses me in the meantime—and I'm pretty certain that this week, I'll come back even stronger.

"*...am I... interrupting you?*" Vera asks politely, when I pick up but don't say a word.

"Oh, no—" I lie, forcing composure where none exists. I had already forgotten I had picked up a call, since no one made a sound on the other end. "How can I help you?"

"*I know it hasn't quite been two weeks like you recommended,*" she begins. "*...but could you perhaps fit me in today or tomorrow?*"

Casting a glance at my phone's screen to check the time, I bring it back to my ear.

"Today would be fine," I say. "If the skin has healed enough. But what's the rush?"

She goes quiet, and the spark in her presence fades in an instant.

"*I'll...*" she says hesitantly. "*I'll explain when I see you.*"

"Alright, give me an hour or so. You know where to find me," I say, my mind whirling with her mystery.

"*See you, Bart,*" she says and hangs up.

I furrow my brow. Her voice seemed... weaker. Like age has at last taken its toll on her. I think about the name that used to be on my neighbour's door. *V. Matani.* I never once considered who it was, but as I dig out the copy of Vera's contract, it is signed with the same name.

Vera Matani.

When her soft knock on the door stirs me into motion, I unlock it and welcome her inside. When we lock eyes, I am shocked to see how wilted she appears. Her poise remains, and her posture is unmistakable—but the sparkle in her eyes has faded. She's holding a potted plant, with lush green leaves and a white flower poking from a stem in the middle. It seems mockingly vibrant in her arms.

"My dear," she says, forcing a smile. "Thank you for making time for me."

I gesture for her to take a seat while I prepare my tools. She places the plant on the floor with unsteady hands, and takes a seat.

"I know you are wondering—" she says, breaking the tension. "Why I'm in such a hurry."

I nod, genuinely worried.

"Are you okay?"

The tattoo machine is in my hand, ready to get to work, but it suddenly feels strangely awkward to hold. I wonder about all the times we must have been no more than a single wall apart, living adjacent lives.

"Although I've known for a while that something was wrong." She clutches the hem of her shirt tighter, taking in a shallow breath. "I decided to let nature do its thing rather than fight it."

"How so?" I say with hoarse uncertainty.

"The doctor told me my cancer has spread to my lungs," she confesses, the words spilling out like they were written with ink in thin air. I can see every letter as they are etched into existence. I notice how strained her every breath appears; a slight tremble in her chest that extends into her hands as they rest in her lap. I am honestly baffled that I didn't notice anything during her first visit. Her gaze drifts off, out towards the horizon beyond the rooftops. "Your work has helped me come to terms with my eventual peril. My impending fate will be beautiful now—cherished rather than abandoned in dirt." She pressed her lips together before parting them, and continues with a faint smile. "I never liked graveyards, anyway. My ashes will be spread across the gorgeous Mediterranean sea by my children. And well—you will take good care of what remains."

Hesitating for a moment, I try to come up with something to match her archaic wisdom.

"I am just a means to your end," I say, drawing a lighter expression on her features. "I will do my best to keep your memory alive."

"I trust you will." Her faint smile grows tight. The display case looms behind her, a physical manifestation of her future. We look at each other for a moment, and I feel her studying my face. "Shall we?" she inquires, regaining her composure slightly.

"Sure."

I get to work, colouring the gentle flowers in shades of Spring; marking a new era for her soul to enter. To prosper in.

"Once upon a time," she begins, as though telling a tale. "I was promised fame and fortune by a man much beyond my years." The sound of the needle buzzing is a soothing backdrop as I let her talk. I keep my eyes on the flowers. They come to life and stretch their stems to bind the goddess in green chains, anchoring her to nature. "But as the years passed and my beauty wilted, my opportunities grew scarce. He abandoned me in Paris for the sake of a younger woman. I had to find my own way in life after that—to look for other means of self-preservation."

"And it all led you straight to me," I say, as I put the final touch on the silky petals of the flowers.

I wonder if these static flowers, imprinted in time, will truly convey her wish. Or if they, too, merely will be viewed as a superficial imitation of mortality.

...

After my session with Vera, I sit for a moment and drink in the stillness. I don't know what it is about her, but she creeps under my skin. Whenever I have inked her, it is as though she has done the same to me. Not with ink, but with words, and a sort of presence only few people possess nowadays. It's like she is determined to claw her way out of the grave before it has even been dug. To never be confined or defined by anything other than herself. I admire that.

Not long after, my manager drops off the supplies for J-Way's tattoo. The package is neatly wrapped in several layers, ensuring safe transportation of the pristine contents. Its lightness seems to lift my spirits, and I glance up at my manager in anticipation of a question I've been wanting to answer for days.

"How do you plan to test this out?" he asks, taking an awkward seat on the bench.

We look at each other for a moment, and I notice how deeply set his eyes are. The frown line between his brows has deepened. The bags underneath the eyes have grown more wrinkly, too.

“I am going to test it on myself,” I reply at last, my pulse quickening at the very thought.

My hands go clammy and I reach for a cigarette just to occupy my fingers.

I don’t have any tattoos myself. No artist has ever been a worthy candidate for decorating my skin. I am like a brand new canvas; pure and untouched.

He raises a brow.

“Well, let me know how it goes,” he says, showing off his teeth in a concerned grimace. He checks his watch before standing. “I gotta run.”

Slightly confused by his unimpressed remark, I begin unwrapping the supplies. When the door closes behind him, I weigh the package in my hands one more time—*is it a burden, or is it a weight that will strengthen my position?*

As I peel each layer off the package, it seems to grow heavier, rather than lighter. The paper shimmers with vows of amplification. Of unthinkable ingenuity.

The tattoo machine smells like iron. The needles—one for me, and two for J-Way, just in case—are slightly larger than my usual.

These are going to hurt.

The gold dust and the transparent ink are separated into two containers. A warning on the gold states I must wear gloves and a respirator when handling the product.

Wearing a pair of black rubber gloves, I clear an area of my desk and wipe it down with antiseptic. It stings in my eyes and nose; a warning of pain to come.

My sketches are spread out in a religious formation, not unlike the biblical angels, all with a variety of piercing eyes that seem to shift and flicker in the harsh light. I spend a while considering which will be worthy, but none of them seem quite right. Some of them even seem... *off.*

I begin sketching obsessively. Eye after eye after eye. Looks that pierce through the paper. Eyes that cry. Eyes that bleed. I feel the art-filled walls of my studio observing me, judging me. It's too much—so I get up, and stride across the studio before taking a stance in front of a self-portrait. The longer I look at it, the more menacing it becomes. There's no movement—of course—but it feels like there might as well be. I can't shake the feeling of its eyes locking in on me whenever I turn my back, so I flip it. I flip the remaining two portraits of artists long gone, too. With their eyes against the wall, I continue sketching.

When at last, I am satisfied with every curve and line, I bring a small container to the table and pour just enough ink for a patch test. I put on a N95 and turn on my desk lamp.

The gold flickers as it catches the light. I angle it back and forth to admire its sheen.

Using the end of a sterile metal spoon, I gently pick up a tiny amount. As I combine the elements I feel like a daring alchemist.

Perhaps I am.

I lean back, hesitating, observing.

Like molten lava, the pool of gold seems alive. It shimmers with an otherworldly fluorescence, a fey uncanniness.

I pick up my design and place it on my forearm. I glide my hand over the stencil in a slow, ritualistic manner, pressing it against my skin before pulling it off. Steam rises around the stencil eye in wicked swirls, ready to be gilded; but as I begin to feel the sting before the needle has even touched my skin, I pause.

Coward, someone whispers. *Coward.*

I flick my head in the direction of the formless voice, flinching at the sound.

There's no one here.

In defiance, I bring out my regular gun, outlining the design carefully but swiftly. My senses betray me, delaying the pain as though it wasn't even my skin at all.

I get it, I think. *I get why this pain is worth it.*

When I am done, I switch to the new machine. There is no time to wait for a healed result. Time belongs to people who earn it—and all I have is a theory. Theories need to be tested.

I wonder silently how the tabloids will react if I succeed—but even more so if I fail. I cast a glance around the studio, then out at a sky tinged with brimming clouds. As the sky darkens further, a glimpse of my feverish body being wheeled into an emergency room, harsh lights bearing down on my body in hues of pale blue, is followed by the same vision, *but with J-Way as the victim.*

I won't do this to you, man.

I have to do it to myself.

The pain is immediate, *intense*, as I hold the gold-filled gun above the tattoo. The pain flickers in and out of an unconscious state, like the eye can sense it will soon be brought to life.

Will it ever forgive me for this sin?

My armpits are soaked despite the cool, stale air of the studio. I force my eyes shut, gritting my teeth as the pain continues to arrive in growing waves.

It needs to be done.

Now.

The needle comes to life, breaking the surface of my skin. A high-pitched noise pierces my ears, like an ancient soul is trying to break free from within me. As the sting subsides, it gives way to an almost euphoric burn. I am thorough, my eyes going dry from staring unblinkingly. With every line, a part of my humanity is replaced by something... *more.*

Something grander.

Now incandescent with gold, the eye is staring back at *me*. We look at each other, and I welcome it to the world of the living, placing the gun gently on the table before observing the impossible.

As the crushed ore settles in my flesh, the line between art and artist blurs and mingles. I ascend into new realms, my soul anchored by intoxicating golden chains.

I will never be alone in my flesh again.

This isn't just a tattoo.

I have always been above ink.

9: A VESSEL

I stare at my burning scar. Its edges seem to glow in unnatural hues of red and black, alarming and distorted. It feels as though the eye follows my every movement. Judging me. Encouraging a deeper exploration of the meaning of art.

Is this a revelation?

...or have I traded in my soul for the sake of creation?

I text my manager a photo of the finished result, my crimson wall a backdrop of reflected pain. No words are attached. None would do it justice.

An unusual fatigue washes over my body. It pulls me under, drowning the last of my obscure humanity. I kill the cruel, revealing lights and retract into the shadows of my backroom. I can always depend on the darkness to welcome me back when I have no other paths left to turn to.

My phone buzzes me back to life after an unknown amount of time. My manager is ecstatic, and I can hear him pacing back and forth.

"*So, it really works?*" he says in a tone of childlike surprise.

I nod as though he would be able to see it.

"It will look more seamless on a healed canvas. Just let J-Way know I'm ready for him."

"*Oh, this is splendid!*" he replies. "*In fact, he is already on his way.*"

I pull the phone away from my ear to check the time, and sure enough, it's nearly 10am. I hang up without further comments, tossing my phone on the curled-up bedsheets. There are bloody stains; tiny specks of red against the dirty off-white.

The drain in the shower stinks from lack of use. As I brush my teeth, the burning sensation on my forearm returns. I spit out the toothpaste and stare at the tattoo reflected in the mirror.

The red, slightly swollen outline hisses at me, the eye narrowing until only a sliver of gold is visible. My heart pounds in my chest and I clench my teeth in pain. I hold back a scream as it twists and rolls back into my skin. For a moment, sheer panic floods my system. I pull at my hair, twisting my neck, wanting to free myself from my skin.

Have I gone mad?

I don't have time for madness.

Sweat pours down my forehead, and with a final, burning flash, I yelp at my reflection.

The tattoo has healed.

I blink, looking back and forth between my face in the mirror, and the pristine tattoo on my forearm. Drenched in feverish sweat, the doorbell buzzes me back to my senses. My chest heaves as I wipe my face. The doorbell buzzes again, this time chiming twice. *Impatiently.* I pull on a sweater from my drawer and enter the studio to let in my client. Right before I open, though, I catch a few words from the other side.

"There's still time to drop this," the bodyguard says in a hushed voice. "Skip the gold, you know the risks."

"I'm not doing tha—."

I unlock the door before J-Way can finish his sentence. J-Way's bodyguard steps inside with long, determined steps and scans the studio before nodding his approval. The rapper strides in, grinning from ear to ear.

"Big day, big man." He laughs, completely untouched by my blank expression. "Let me see the ink. I'm *buzzing* to get started."

I grab a mask, and with a hand on the back of my desk chair, I pull it out to take a seat. My hands tremble slightly as I pull on the gloves and pick up the container.

Good thing I won't be doing detailed work today.

J-Way lingers behind me, wavering, awaiting a glimpse of his gold.

No, *my* gold.

He is just a canvas.

I glance up at him once before I open the ink bottle. Sweat continues to pearl at my temples. I pour the pale, translucent liquid into the mixing bowl and tap out a tiny amount of gold, stirring between each tap.

Tap, tap, tap.

I stir again, and J-Way lets go of a deep breath.

"We're really doing this," he says enigmatically. "Do you think it's going to work?"

Turning to face him, I place a hand on my sleeve, with the intention of revealing my secret, but something halts me.

"It will," I simply reply, but my hands grow clammy under the black rubber gloves.

"I'm already writing a song about it," he adds, pulling off his t-shirt. "I'm thinking about the hook line. Something like... *Embellished and adorned, my pride can now be worn, mortality is buried now, ready, set, let's mourn,*" his voice laced with a South African twang, the rhythm bouncing off the bare walls of the studio.

I catch my head bopping up and down to the beat, even after his words fade out.

"Not bad," I admit, thankful for the distraction. "Wanna get started?"

His eyes twinkle with delight as he gets into position.

"Mind if we listen to my latest album while you work?" he asks. "I've rearranged the sequence and need to practice the setup in my head."

I nod, bringing the mixing bowl onto my sterile tabletop. I turn on the needle just as he presses play on his phone.

"Adding the sound of your machine to the new single would be dope, I'm telling you," he says. "I'll totally do that."

As I add the gold to the tip, my vision blurs slightly. I take a steadying breath and recover my poise. The music seems to distort like I have been plunged underwater. I think about the strange voice that seemed to appear when I was sketching. Of the tattoo. Of everything I've set in motion.

With every stroke, I feel more feverish. I keep zoning out, shaking my head to stay focused. J-Way starts recording the sound of the tattoo gun, then replays it to himself.

"Yeah, this will be sick."

By the end of the session, as gold foils in every crevice of the design, I instinctively pull off my sweater and dry my face once more. I down a glass of water, and as J-Way sits up, my dizziness overwhelms me. I slump back onto the chair, seeing double. I try to focus on J-Way, but his two forms keep splitting and merging back together.

Luckily J-Way is far too invested in his own reflection to notice my distress.

Or my tattoo.

I watch as they drive off, before dragging my feet across the polished floor towards my backroom. My fatigue is weighing on me like lead, my vision hazy around the edges as though the low-hanging fog from the street had seeped through the gaps in the windows.

The moment I close the door behind me, though, the room lights up in flashes as notifications arrive on my phone. It's lying face up on the dirty sheet, providing glimpses of pale blue light that cast irregular shadows on the bare walls. Some shadows flicker, while others linger and grow darker. I grab the cool phone and roll onto my side, watching the world react to the news of the gold embedded in their favourite rapper.

I accept the collaboration invitation on J-Way's post immediately. The rush of scrolling through the comments keeps me awake for hours, my eyes growing puffy and dry. Seeing 20.000 new followers roll in in the span of hours is thrilling. When I finally try to sleep, though, it's already evening, and my stomach growls like a snarling dog.

I force my three eyes shut, and count my sheep.

INTERLUDE: I SEE PORTENTS

A few sleepless days later, I get a call from J-Way.

"*Not to sound paranoid, but—*" J-Way's voice is laced with an unusual urgency. "*But I think I'm being followed.*"

Rosaline, I think. She must have a hand in this.

"What are you talking about?" I say in a casual tone.

Maybe *too* casual.

"*It might just be in my head, you know—knowing how valuable the new ink is and all that,*" he says. "*Everyone knows where I am all the time. Maybe I shouldn't be posting on my story in real time.*"

"I'm sure your bodyguard is taking good care of you," I lie. "Just relax, he knows what he's doing. Post whenever."

"*Anyway,*" he murmurs. "*Sorry to have wasted your time, I just... didn't know who else to call.*"

"All good," I reply, but he grows quiet on the other end of the line.

After several seconds, the sound of shuffling feet is followed by a prolonged silence.

A door slams.

Something breaks.

The line goes dead.

I wonder if that was the last time I ever heard from him.

10: BYE-BYE

I stare at the ended call until the screen turns off, and my own, partial reflection is plastered onto the dark glass. I know what I told Rosaline—and I know she keeps her promises. Seeing it unfold in real time should be more disturbing than it is, though.

An involuntary yawn forces my tense jaw to release. My whole body gives in, stretching my sore and stiff limbs. In the bathroom, I shave meticulously despite the overwhelming fatigue.

The bar awaits.

Grabbing my keys and wallet, I remind myself to run the vacuum when I return. The dust bunnies in the corners of the studio are growing ears. It's ridiculous—I can't postpone the cleaning any longer. But before I can leave, I realise that the plant Vera brought is still sitting on the floor along the wall. The leaves have started to droop, and I feel a sudden flicker of pity for the useless thing. I pick it up and place it on the windowsill, then offer it a bit of water from a bottle that's been standing on my desk for days.

At last, I dash downstairs, passing one of my neighbours without a second glance. I cross the street as though I am invincible, and someone slams their brakes, cursing me through their windshield.

Glad I never believed in curses.

Inside the bar, my usual bartender is pouring a pint for a woman sitting next to a man wearing a bowler hat. I avoid the seats next to them and find a table by myself.

The bartender finishes chatting with the woman, before sliding onto the seat across the round table. It wobbles, the tiles below it slightly uneven.

"I saw a picture of the golden tattoo," she whispers, leaning in. A loose strand of hair falls in front of her face and she swiftly tucks it behind her ear. "I honestly didn't believe it at first... but you did it." The unknown man in the bowler hat twists in his seat ever so slightly, side-eyeing our conversation. His presence is unsettling, for whatever reason. "I'll definitely come by the gallery when he's modelling. It's just brilliant," she adds, and I force a smile on my face to please her. It's strange having her sit across from me. Like we know each other. "Anyway, Mr. Pioneer, what's on your plate today?"

"The usual, I suppose," I reply, and she sets off towards the kitchen to get my food.

I realise that she in fact does know me. Perhaps better than anyone else. My routines are entwined with hers, and a sort of symbiosis has formed between us. In a sense, we're both disposable. Just playing our part in a fabricated ecosystem. But I like it like that.

Just as she returns, one of J-Way's songs comes on the radio. The man pays for his drinks and right before he leaves, he turns to me. The tattoo shifts on my arm, the pain shooting through my body.

One of his eyes is gone.

Several seconds pass while his hollow gaze is fixed on me—he doesn't speak, doesn't even blink. It is as though the sounds around us fade, the lights dimming. A faint, dull scent emanates from his parted lips, and with his yellowing teeth exposed, he is frightening. Where his other eye once must have been, uneven scar tissue is stretched across the area.

My forearm burns, but I keep a straight face and clench my teeth.

Who is that?

Without further notice, he exits through the swinging door. All sounds return to normal and the light from the lamp on the wall grows brighter.

The rotten stench stays behind in the air like a phantom of his presence, though, forcing me to hold back a gag. As I wait for it to be swept away by the current of the aircon, the pain in my arm finally fades once more.

I eat mechanically to the tune of a mediocre pop song. Every bite seems to cling to my tightening throat, so I wash them down with another beer before bolting out of the bar. I can feel the bartender's eyes on me as I leave, but I don't look back.

Pouncing up the steps to the fourth-floor studio, I toss my coat on the bench before running a hand down my face.

I still feel unwell, like I might have a mild case of the flu. I haven't slept in two days, and in the corners of my vision, strange outlines of dark figures flicker. It's obvious I need sleep.

I don't need a visual reminder.

At first, they come and go. Flickering, partial shapes hover around me, clad in ragged, hooded robes. I take a step back, holding my breath, my eyes darting between them. Little by little, they seem to settle; fixing themselves in the frame of my vision, like ornamentation on an old scripture.

It is your fault, one of them whispers.

I stiffen. No matter where I look, they darken, like acknowledging their presence widens the gateway between the underworld and mine. Like the two are merging.

You let him in, they chime in a chilling choir.

No.

I look down at my hands.

...or did I?

Who is he?

My eyes follow the vein in the palm of my hand, up towards the golden eye. As I run my thumb over it, I can sense the figures nodding. Soon, they begin whispering, like they might disturb a sleeping entity.

...but it seems that that might already be too late.

In denial, I decide to busy myself with the vacuum, which in turn drowns out the whispers—but as I push the vacuum over the rug, not a single sound of dirt whirls through the neck. I turn off the machine and open it to check the bag, scowling.

It's full of dust and dirt.

When I look at the corner of the studio, the dust bunnies are gone.

I swear they were there earlier.

I swear.

I shake my head and turn off the light to protect myself from the looming presences. The darkness swallows their silhouettes like a gaping black hole. I breathe quietly in the darkness for a moment, but the sound of my heartbeat begins to throb in my ear. I feel a breath against my neck, one that isn't mine—and the chill of an open window that doesn't exist.

Bye-bye, a voice whispers, and the sensations evaporate at once.

Whatever gateway I opened, I hope there's a way to close it again for good.

I collapse onto the bed, for now.

During the night, I'm plagued by disturbing inner monologues that seem to go on and on, keeping my mind at the edge of sleep. I have repeated visions of crowded walls with rotting pieces of skin nailed to them. Of framed paintings of men flipping themselves back and forth, like they're playing a messed up game of peekaboo.

It's in my hands, it's in my hands, it's in my hands. But at what cost, but at what cost, but at what cost.

In the morning, even the icy water pouring from the shower head doesn't make a dent in my fatigue. I drag myself around, preparing for yet another client, but I feel apathetic, my hands trembling uncontrollably.

Whenever I pull up my sleeve, even just for a moment, an overwhelming nausea strikes as the tattoo threatens to split my skin in half.

It healed, yes.

But it also evolved.

...

The young woman at my door is adamant about entering when she sees my feverish face—but curiosity quickly gets the better of her.

"Amanda," I say. "Take a seat."

We briefly discuss the contract before her crooked signature is dotted on the bottom right corner. It's simple enough; her skin belongs to me, so she can't get the tattoo removed or altered. She has to model for me at least once a year, and when she passes away, the tattoo will be preserved and exhibited in my name. Most importantly, this is a non-reversible contract. She tells me that her friend is modelling for me, and I welcome her to the team.

I have a design ready for her already—one I've been holding onto for a while. It is a meadow with a fawn in the centre, slightly smaller than my usual sketches. Looking at it relieves my unease, and I manage to place the stencil and get to work.

The session drags out as my forearm keeps throbbing. Outside, a dog is barking and the late afternoon traffic is sending hues of red taillights twinkling through the studio curtains. The shadow of a bus passing down in the street glides across the wall in front of me.

Whenever I narrow my eyes, the fawn seems to shift its weight on the moss beneath its hooves. Perplexed, I shield it with my hand as I work on outlining a tree instead.

About an hour later, I'm satisfied with the progress. The dark ink sheen on her back is eye-catching.

"All done for—" I say, my voice hoarse, so I clear my throat a few times. "All done for today."

I wrap her up and we shake hands before I send her off into the evening. The shadowy figures reappear in my field of vision, so I bury myself in my sketchbooks, aiming to find solace in my own creativity. But as I look through the sketches I intended to continue, they're all looking...

different. One in particular stands out; completely finished in a way I don't recall.

11: TAINTED IDIOMS

My manager barges into the studio without knocking, his grim expression an omen of doom.

Not impending.

Doom is at my door.

"You must have read the headlines," he says. "Seen the news—hell, just look out of your window."

I shake my head. He is vexed, with wide eyes and a crooked tie.

"I have, in fact, *not*," I admit.

It's 10pm and I've been sketching frantically with sleep-deprived strokes since I finished my session with the new client. Yesterday seems like it happened weeks ago, and at the same time—like it still hasn't ended. Even though the shadows left, I can almost feel a slight, incorporeal breeze, like a door has been left slightly ajar.

At my manager's request, I get to my feet and open the window. As soon as I do, the paparazzi start flashing their cameras down in the crowded street. A beam of light is directed towards me immediately, harsh and unrelenting. I pull back and draw the curtains in one motion, my heart thudding in my chest.

"What is going on?"

"You might want to see that for yourself," he says, and gestures towards my PC.

I log in and search the news while hovering over the desk. My back hurts, and my manager is tapping his fingers impatiently on the table.

A photo of J-Way is on the front page of several newspapers with a variation of the same headline:

'*Ripped apart and left to bleed: World-famous rapper brutally murdered and robbed of his own skin*' and '*The price of immortality: J-Way mutilated in his own home*'

"We have to publish a statement—" my manager says, before I can form a coherent response. "Stating how deeply sorry we are to hear about his passing," he continues. "But we also need to make it clear that the artwork must be returned to you immediately."

The words on the screen go blurry in my vision. My chest tightens, nausea striking at the thought of the crime—but another part of me wants to ask the question:

Where is the tattoo now?

"Obviously, but—" I say, my eyes still glued to the screen.

I'm still not sure how Rosaline got me to agree to this. She has been fueling my greed and hunger for power—now she's feeding me the results.

I asked for more, but... did I kill J-Way in the process?

I think about his last words, the splintered self confidence in his tone of voice.

"Get your coat," he says urgently, pulling me out of the studio by the sleeve. "If we don't act now, decay will smoulder our efforts. It's now or never. We're meeting with Rosaline right after."

Decay, I think, as we step onto the sidewalk. The acrid stench lingers in my vicinity as a constant reminder.

The crowd of journalists from various media stations begin their spitfire interrogation under the pale street lights. My manager steps forward with a raised hand to signal a ceasefire.

As every microphone is propped in his direction, the loud voices hush in anticipation of his words. A sense of deep foreboding forms as a noose around my neck. I take a few steadying breaths, but I can't help shivering.

And they notice immediately.

"In the light of recent events," he begins. "We would like to send our deepest condolences to the parents of the deceased—" I curl my fingers at the avoidance in his rehearsed speech. "...as well as make it clear that the artwork on said deceased belongs to Bart Giovanni. He is the rightful owner as stated by the signed *and eternally binding* contract."

A few gasps are quickly followed by rapid questions, the flash of cameras and waves of murmurs. The wind rustles the barren trees, and stirs the piles of fallen leaves.

"What is your next move?" someone shouts above the wind as it begins to pick up.

My manager clears his throat, and the clouds above us darken as though even the moon had dipped below the horizon. In mourning, they shed a few tears on the crowd.

"We urge the thief to hand over the artwork immediately to avoid deterioration of the..." he pauses slightly, hesitating. "Organic materials." A few muffled questions overlap each other, clouding coherence. An image of J-Way's skin displayed side by side with my existing artwork flashes like old film in front of my eyes, flicking between different angles of the same scene. "It must be handled correctly and preserved with great care by professional hands," he continues. "To ensure its preservation, we are offering a... substantial bounty for its safe return. That is all, thank you."

A car pulls up by the crowded sidewalk, and my manager attempts to guide me inside. Instead, I'm shaking violently, my body betraying me at last.

"*What* are you waiting for?" my manager exclaims in exasperation.

What do I even say?

A way out?

Behind the wheel, Rosaline is wearing dark shades, the heavy frames resting on the bridge of her nose.

"If you don't try, there's no champagne," she says, the encouraging Italian idiom suddenly tainted with something much darker.

The sound of the blinker and the soft, orange light from the dashboard chips away at my sanity.

Blink.

How did she coerce me...

Blink.

...to go along with this?

Blink.

"Whe-where are we going?" I stammer, even though I'd rather not be going at all.

"We're meeting with the middle man of the middle man," she says enigmatically. "Don't worry, my guys are on the case."

My lips part as though I had the guts to ask who those guys are. I close them again as she glances over her shoulder. Not at me—but at the cars behind us. Reflected in her shades is a world tinted by hues of grey. A world that passes by on its own, containing a set of intricate games I'll never know the rules to.

My manager sighs in a constrained, rhythmic pattern, fidgeting with his phone as the screen keeps lighting up with incoming calls.

"Here we are," Rosaline says in delight, parking on a narrow lane between two ancient buildings. A dark figure gestures for us to enter through the back door. It's the backroom of a restaurant in central Milan—the sound of plates clinking muffling our murmured conversation. "Where is it now?" Rosaline demands, tapping her wristwatch.

"In the back of a cooled, unmarked truck, near the southern border of Tanzania, miss."

Rosaline casts a critical glance into the kitchen. The staff are bustling about at high speed, not paying her a moment of their time. They're probably running the final service of the night right now.

"Bart, we need the address of the trusted conservatory that procured your framed artwork," she says, turning to me.

"They're in the US," I say.

"I know they're in the US—I just need to know which state to guide my team to."

"What will they do?" I ask. "I really don't get where this is heading, hasn't it been stolen?"

A hush of cool autumn air breaks the damp tension as one of the kitchen staff brushes past us to toss away some trash. It smells like seafood.

Empty shells, hollowed out with force.

Rosaline pauses, but only until the man has returned to the kitchen.

"Stolen by my guys, yes," she says. My jaw goes slack in awe. "Now they're going to be arrested by my *other* guys. Then they'll ship it off for conservation, and *voilà*—it'll be returned to your studio within a week."

Faint laughter of merry guests seeps through the kitchen from the restaurant out front. Shifting my weight, I lean a hand on the steel tabletop next to me. She hands me a torn piece of paper and clicks the back of a pen on the countertop.

"The address," she commands, and as I am about to double-check the address on my phone, she pulls it from my grasp. She taps away on the keyboard, scrunching her face. When she hands it back, the browser looks different. "Better safe than sorry," she muses as I find the address. I scratch it down and Rosaline slips it to the guy. "One week," she says. "Best to keep your head down in the meantime."

12: PUNCH AFTER PUNCH

The following day, I'm hunched in front of my computer, curtains drawn. My Chinese takeaway box has gone cold, and the entire evening has vanished in a blur of news articles.

One particular image of me standing between my models at the gallery with the headline: '*Who's next?*' is striking—but when I see the next headline, my gut plummets.

'*Model of famous tattoo artist reveals the details of debated contract: "I want out"*'

I quickly press the link and see an image of Amanda. I scowl, pushing back in my chair to cross my arms over my chest.

There's no such thing as backing out, I think bitterly. *You signed a contract.*

The parents of the deceased client are already enough legal work to deal with, my manager having pulled them into court to confront them with the signed contract their son agreed to.

It worked, though.

The wailing of an ambulance rushing by is followed by quick flashes of blue light. It stirs me out of my slump and I finish my noodles and the remaining spring roll.

Right before I go to bed, I find my finger hovering over the refresh button. I linger, but my urge washes me away with the tide of endless information.

I reload the news page one last time.

'*BREAKING NEWS: Remains of Famous Rapper Resurface in Tanzania*'

Before I can react, my manager is on the line. I pick up the call.

"*Station One has invited you to an interview tomorrow morning. You will agree.*"

"I, I—" I stammer, as the looming shadows appear around me and lean in.

You're in deep waters, they whisper, their voices overlapping.

I clench my eyes shut until my eyeballs hurt.

"*7:30am, radio interview. Your driver will pick you up at 6:20,*" my manager states coldly; I can almost sense the tightness in his jaw. See the river of urgency in his eyes. "*And remember,*" he adds. "*You are grateful for its safe return.*"

...

At dawn I'm pacing the sidewalk in my shades and an oversized hoodie; a weak attempt at obscuring my identity.

I hope it'll do.

My driver pulls up, and I hurry inside the sleek car. The seat is warm, and the sun has barely gotten ahold of Milan yet as we head towards central.

Cars line each side of the narrow street, and my driver flicks on the emergency flash as he slows down to let me out in the middle of the early morning traffic. I step through the gap between two parked cars before the bouncer of Studio One lets me inside.

I take a seat in the lounge, but a clerk swiftly guides me towards the recording studio. With each step, my heart sinks further.

The studio doors slide open, and a deafening, muffled sensation presses in on me from the dark acoustic panels lining every wall. I take a seat as instructed and the host gets straight to the point.

"In light of recent accusations of opportunism from the press, and the remarkable retrieval of rapper J-Way's stolen tattoo, we're pleased to welcome renowned tattoo artist, Bart Giovanni, to the studio," the host's voice whips, slashing through the air without reverberating. It sends a chill down my spine—one that makes me deeply aware of how I breathe. "So, Bart—what started this... fascination of yours? What's it like building your name on a taboo?"

I stiffen, as the red light switches on in front of me, signalling that my mic is live.

Think.

"My dad left nothing behind," I begin, trying to make amends, but the stagnant air of the room tightens my throat. "I realised that I'd never want to be forgotten," I continue. "Turns out, a lot of people share that wish."

"And J-Way sought you out for this reason?" he asks.

"He liked pushing boundaries, just like me," I reply, avoiding his scrutinising glare.

"You are profiting from a murder. How do you justify this... transaction?" he says in a flat tone. "Do you truly believe it is ethical?"

I swallow my urge to lash back at him, sinking my index finger into the cushion of my seat in frustration. He raises his brows with a blank expression, awaiting my response.

Exhaling through my nose, I measure my words carefully.

"Everything comes at a price," I reply with forced control. "If you pay to be immortalised, that's what you'll get. I'm just a vessel for that opportunity. There are limited options."

Immediately, the host's face turns wicked. A triumphant smile spreads, showing off impeccably aligned teeth.

"But not zero," he says with a hint of mystery.

I scrunch my face quizzically, but he pauses before elaborating.

"How so?" I ask.

"You have a rival, whether you like it or not."

Before I can ask who he's talking about, the host turns off the microphone and a song fades into my headphones. He casts a mischievous look at me across the desk, where microphones and PC screens fill the space between us. But there's more; a sense of foreboding builds, *simmering*, and sweat pearls on my temples.

The lyrics to J-Way's new single, *Golden Immortality,* writhe their claws into my skull.

"*Long live me, guess I'll live long,*" the ghost of J-Way sings, and the host turns up the volume until my eardrums threaten to burst. "*Watch how I thrive with my name on your tongue.*"

Without thinking, I pull off the headphones and stumble out of the studio, my steps heavy with fury. The staff glare at me, some even trying to get in my way—but I don't look back.

...

My driver has been looping around the block for about half an hour, waiting for me to emerge from my humiliating exposition.

When he notices me, he pulls over and I get in.

He shoots me a sidelong look while merging back into the slow traffic.

"Did they cut you off?" he asks, glancing briefly at the radio which hums with the tune of a top-charting boy band. I shake my head, leaning back in my seat. "I guess that means you didn't hear about the skeletons, then," he says, without looking at me.

My shock fixes me in place for a split second. It's so rare for him to talk to me directly that his voice sounds foreign to me.

"What!?" I burst out, as Milan glides by carelessly.

"The artist," he continues. "Who's painting skeletons. I think you set some post-mortem trends in motion."

I blink feverishly, every passing stranger blurring around the edges, like humanity just entered a new era—*an era, where death is just a new beginning*.

13: HE WAS RIGHT HERE

The café looks alarmingly bright, gleaming in the sunlight as my driver drops me off. I shudder and retreat across the street to my studio, but as I reach the fourth floor, something—or rather, *someone*—is standing in front of the door. At first I wave them off as an apparition of my paranoia, *but then they turn to face me.*

For a moment, we merely stare at each other. Perplexed, I realise that only one eye is staring back at me; *I've seen him before.*

The one-eyed man lifts his chin at me, the walls of the hallway suddenly closing in.

"Show me your arm," he demands coldly, his stiff, dark suit fit for a funeral.

With a trembling hand, I curl my fingers around the edge of my sleeve.

When I hesitate, he clenches his fists.

"*Show me.*" His hollow voice doesn't echo as he repeats himself. *Instead, it pierces through me.* As I mechanically reveal my golden secret, its chatoyancy seems more pronounced than ever before, the gold hardening beneath my skin. The faint glow grows in strength until the gold begins stretching itself like creeping vines extending from the tattoo. I wince and twist my fingers in agony, but the man merely shakes his head. "Like you said," he drones. "Everything in life comes at a cost."

He takes a step forward, directly at me. I swerve, but not quite enough to avoid him.

The cold touch of his form doesn't brush past me—*it walks straight through me.* I turn to watch him as he shuffles down the stairs, his footsteps as silent as the grave.

I whip down my sleeve, a shuddering gasp stunting my breath. When I hear the door closing at ground level, I unlock the studio and hurry to the window to ensure he doesn't linger. As he strolls down towards the end of the road with the sun at his back, my guts churn at the realisation; *he doesn't cast a shadow on the pavement.*

Pulling at my hair, I take five long strides across the room to double check if my door is locked. Although it is, the knowledge doesn't settle my nauseating anxiety. A door won't keep him, or rather—*it*—away. Nothing will.

I feel exposed, like I have become an object of scrutiny, merging with my art. My tattoo throbs with every thud of my beating heart as my thoughts loop around the same question.

Wasn't this what I wanted all along?

To become something beyond mere flesh?

And wait—*bones*. *Skeletons*. I have those piled in my closet. Maybe those painted skeletons will soften the edges of the public's morality—even out the grey—until the lines of ethics have blurred and vanished.

...

Much to my own dismay, I find no rest in sketching like I usually would. The pen meets the paper, but every time I attempt to draw a line, my forearm burns and hisses in protest. My vision distorts the already uneven outline, but I continue trying until the pain becomes unbearable, forcing the pencil so viciously it snaps. The pencil tip rolls off the sketchbook, leaving behind a dusty trail of graphite.

I rip off my hoodie in one motion and toss it on the studio floor.

"What do you want!?" I exclaim, the eye staring back at me unblinking.

Long strands of gold now extend down my wrist and up my bicep, like glorified sepsis. In response, it stretches further, creeping ever so slightly.

I pull myself upright but the dizziness is overwhelming.

What do I do now?

As my bicep is suffused with gold against my will, I shake my arm vigorously as though to shed the festering monstrosity.

"Stop!" I beg the gold. "Please, stop!"

At last, it settles into my flesh, the pain subsiding. I can taste the ore in my mouth—it has a metallic tang, much like blood.

My chest still heaves with distress when I pull my hoodie back on and check my watch. The bar opens in an hour, so I light a cigarette with trembling hands and lean on my window frame to observe the passersby down below.

If he got into this world, there must be a way out again.

There's one for all of us.

My phone buzzes in my pocket with an incoming call, but I shrug it off as I exhale into the cool autumn air. Dark clouds gather on the horizon, promising rain to the fading patches of grass around the city centre. When the phone buzzes again, the short vibration seems gentler, more familiar—so I check the screen.

It's Vera.

She has sent me an email, so I leave her call unanswered.

'*Dearest Bart,*

The weather is quite unpleasant today, although I doubt that interests you much. I simply wanted to apologise for rejecting your invitation to model at the next exhibition, but I assure you we will be reunited once again soon enough. Take care of the plant for me. It's a peace lily—hard to kill. I forgot to mention it was a present.

Love,

Vera'

Reunited soon enough.

I touch the leaves of the plant, rubbing one gently between my fingers. The flower has already started to brown at the edges, and the scent of decay blends alarmingly indistinguishably with the flower and the soil.

With the wind picking up, I decide to leave for the bar early to avoid the rain. When I enter, the bartender is sweeping the floor, preparing for her shift.

"Hey buddy," she chirps, but her expression quickly falters. "Tough day? I heard you were on the radio this morning, but I slept through my alarm." I slump down on a chair by the counter without answering her question. "No offence, but you look like you haven't slept in a week," she adds, tossing the contents of the duster pan into a bin before grabbing me a pint.

"I wanted to ask you about a... customer," I murmur, tapping a finger on the counter.

She narrows her eyes at me while the beer gushes through the tap.

"Depends on what you want to know," she replies.

"The other day," I begin, as she hands me the glass. "There was a particular guy, the one with a missing eye? Does he come here often?"

She frowns.

"Never seen a man like that around here, no."

"He was sitting right here," I insist, gesturing at my seat. "You were talking to him, I think, and—"

She laughs, her eyes softening as though finally catching a joke.

There is none.

"Pretty sure I would've remembered that sort of face, it's not something you come across every day."

A ripple of goosebumps flushes across my back.

She didn't see him?

14: DAMAGE CONTROL

Over the course of the weekend, I didn't leave the studio at all, ignoring every text and call, trying to shield myself from the outside world. The rain has been pouring down, pelting against my windows since early morning. I was supposed to finish Amanda's tattoo today, but she has blocked me on all social media platforms, leaving me to question whether tomorrow's client will even show up.

I stare at my walls, the flipped paintings a reminder of the path I have succumbed to. My stack of contracts isn't unlike my mother's unruly pile of unpaid bills either—I can hear her words echo through the generational rift as she comforts me:

What they don't know, won't hurt them.

Sudden footsteps emerge from the other side of the door, thundering up the old staircase.

BANG, BANG, BANG.

A fist pounds on my door, the wood vibrating in its frame.

I freeze until I hear my manager's voice.

"Bart, let me in," he commands.

I wistfully comply under the scrutiny of the dark figures gathering in my peripheral—but just as I place my hand on the doorknob, they interject.

Can't be good news, they whisper. *Don't let him in.*

"Oh, shut up," I exclaim a little too loudly, causing my manager to cease his shuffling-about in the hallway.

"Who are you talking to?" he asks, and I recoil. "*Come ooon*, open the door." I twist the door-handle and my manager pushes through the narrow gap I barely allow, before I swiftly close it behind him. "The artwork is with the conservatory in Dallas as we speak," my manager begins, placing his leather briefcase on the bench as he takes a seat on my chair. "In two days, it'll be on a plane, and by Thursday, it'll be right here with us. Now—we need to plan your next exhibition."

Running a hand down my face, I roll my eyes. There hasn't been a single day to catch my breath since I hired him.

"Can't we just do the same thing as last time, but with J-Wa—I mean, the new artwork as a main feature?"

He sighs in exasperation.

"Oh, this is why you need me. I've had the opportunity to discuss some strategies with the skeleton artist, Rafael. My suggestion is to team up with him, and entwine your success to shed some of the focus on the... tragic passing of your client."

The floorboards creak beneath my manager as he shifts his weight to get off the chair. The creaks seemingly continue despite his lack of movement, as though the building itself is urging him to leave.

But how could he?

We're already in too deep.

I chew the inside of my cheek, gutted by his cruel betrayal. The smoulders of ash in my chest seem to flicker back up in flame.

"You talked to him without discussing it with me first?" I spit, my jaw tightening.

"You might want to answer your phone next time, then." He fires back, "—and *yes*. I'm Rafael's manager, too." *He's what?* The unusual rage nearly fills me to the breaking point, but he continues unfazed. "We are renting a mausoleum for the exhibition next week," he explains. "I'll try to convince your models to show up. Plead with them—wave a contract in their face, or whatever it takes. I'm working on suing Amanda as well; things are in motion." Grabbing the handle of his briefcase once more, he looks me up and down theatrically. "And take a shower, I beg you. See you on Thursday. *Ciao*."

...

The rest of the evening is a blur; the shadows murmur their tyranny at my loss of control as I let the water carry away the past week's grime. The drain sputters in disgust as it swallows the last of my dignity.

Tousling my hair with the towel, I avoid my father's eyes in the mirror, knowing full well that he's watching me slip.

Can't you see I've already achieved what you were never capable of?

He doesn't care, he doesn't care, the voices taunt.

Pushing past the flickering demons with thundering steps, I turn off the lights and head to bed.

In the morning, I put on a fresh set of jeans and a white t-shirt. When I attempt to leave for the café to grab my morning coffee, though, a well-dressed, middle-aged man is at my door, ready for his first appointment. We stare at each other for a moment, before I clear my throat.

It must be that guy who sells art in Switzerland.

"Well," I say in a stutter. "Welcome, I mean."

He simply smiles politely and takes a wordless tour around the studio as I prepare for his session.

My fingers are itching to get to work. Mostly to get control of my spiralling thoughts and zone out for a moment.

God knows I need the break.

As I wipe down the bench and settle into my creaking chair, we exchange an eager look.

"When I saw your exhibition last month," he begins, "I knew I had to be a part of this."

"It's a pleasure having you," I reply, shuffling between my sketches before handing him two I believe would be a good fit. "You work in a gallery, right?"

"I'm a curator, yes," he continues, before glancing at the sketches. The paper rustles slightly, making a crinkling sound. "Can't quite see the appeal of those skeletons. I like the idea of being art, but I want to be around to experience it."

I swallow a lump in my throat at those words, thinking of J-Way and my own, golden secret.

"I get that," I reply awkwardly.

"This one."

He waves the sketch of a Roman empress at the Colosseum with two prancing war-horses towering in front of her. It is part of my historical collection, and I take pride in knowing he chose this particular one.

"Would you ever consider bringing your models to Switzerland?" he asks, just as I am about to begin.

I don't like doing business without my manager. I feel vulnerable in a way—so I consider his question carefully.

"It's complicated," I begin, while staring at the blank skin on his back. A faint, almost translucent scar runs down his neck along the spine. "There's a certain exclusivity to keeping things local. And the models... it's not part of their contract to travel."

"Well, I'll be there," he says cheerfully, before the conversation goes dry and the hum of the needle replaces our words.

I work in relative peace for a solid thirty minutes—but as the first horse comes to life, a sudden, sharp pain in my left forearm makes me push in the needle too forcefully. Something in me wanted to—and I have to force myself backwards to avoid stabbing him again.

The client winces, and the blood begins trickling down his back. The needle stops buzzing as I feverishly grasp for words. My arm is twitching, and my mind spins with the word:

Again. Again. Again.

"God, I'm sorry, I—" I lie, grabbing the paper towel to stop the bleeding. "That has never happened before."

You did that on purpose, the dark figures say as they lean in, examining the wound.

A dark, translucent finger stretches towards the blood, touching it ever so slightly before bringing the finger close to its obscure face. It inhales, then sighs.

"Better take a break if you're not on your A-game," the client says coldly.

I twist my face, humiliation striking.

"I will finish the outline." I insist. "I can do this."

The work resumes without further distractions, and four hours later, the client exits the studio, eternally inked and wrapped in cellophane. I should feel some sense of relief at the sight. Instead, I deflate immediately, dread forcing my body to slump into the desk chair.

This is getting out of hand.

In fact, the sheer embarrassment of screwing up the only thing I'm good at is squeezing out my life force minute by minute as I dissociate. My head is a whirlpool. My flesh is tainted by experimental godhood. And perhaps, my soul has already left.

I attempt to wind down my spiraling thoughts, but the more I suppress them, the louder they become.

What if

I mess up

again?

15: TROPHIES

I heave myself upright and check my phone for the first time in days. Six missed calls from my manager during the weekend, and a follow from Rafael on Instagram. His page is colourful; every painted bone has a strangely cheerful pastel-pattern, a stark juxtaposition to the usual approach to death. I find it invigorating, and somehow not as threatening as I expected.

This is merely a gimmick, I think. *My art takes true skill—even a child could pull this off.*

While I browse his feed, a text from my manager grabs my attention.

"*The truck is nearly there, be ready to let in the artwork.*"

Shoving my phone in my pocket, I trot to the window in the studio and keep my eyes on the road. Not five minutes pass before a big, white truck idles by the entrance to my building. My tattoo is throbbing slightly, but so is my pulse. I let them inside and pull the door wide open.

Two men are carrying a pedestal and I gesture at the bare spot on the floor next to the other frame. They place it gently before shuffling down the stairs to get the art.

My eyes are fixed on the glass frame covered by dark cloth as they manoeuvre it carefully through the door. The second it is placed on the pedestal, they leave without any pleasantries, shutting the door behind them.

The smell of their sweat lingers in the air and an unusual silence follows in their wake. The sound of cars from the street is muffled as though I am wearing earplugs, and the faint beeps of the truck backing up are barely noticeable.

I hesitate briefly, my hand outstretched as though to pull the cloth off—*but before I can make the move, it slides off by itself.*

As the drape swirls to the floor, J-Way's wish to be immortalised stares back at me in golden splendour, the black ink still fresh and opaque. *Strangely so*. My outstretched hand burns as the angry, spidery veins reembark on their quest to map my skin in ore. For once, the burn feels... *euphoric*.

J-Way's words replay in my head, like his records will continue to do on every radio station around the globe:

The pain is just a bonus.

I watch on in fascination as my hand is transformed. It feels stiff, like I am sacrificing mobility to become something greater. *I laugh*. I laugh until my stomach aches. I laugh until I have to bend over to catch my breath.

The looming shadows shudder at my amusement, ceasing their usual, incoherent murmurs. My cheeks hurt from grinning as I pick up the silky drape. It feels like nothing in my golden hand.

I look around the room, and the figures bend at my will one by one. They move out of my line of sight, their gaping mouths gone.

Good.

Finally.

Within the silence, my studio feels larger. My breaths are full and controlled, and my hand feels warm to the touch. I fold the drape neatly and tuck it in a drawer. I adjust my stack of sketches, so the edges are aligned.

Despite the relief, a sudden, unbearable fatigue washes over me. *Even gods have their limits*, I muse, withdrawing to my backroom like the day has already come to an end.

Alas, I wake at 5pm, overcome by hunger. My golden hand gleams in the sterile light of the studio, the veins protruding slightly.

I pull on a pair of gloves before heading to the bar. The street is lined with parked cars, the sky gaping cloudlessly above. Someone's TV is on in a first-floor apartment next to the bar. The window is open, letting the indistinguishable chatter of some entertainment show carry with the breeze.

Given it's the first Thursday of the month, a poorly drawn sign featuring a microphone has been placed out front to signal it's karaoke night.

My breath is visible in the cool air, and as I enter the warm, damp bar, two women are already singing a duet as the words are highlighted across the tiny TV screen on the back wall.

"It's getting colder."

The bartender notes observantly, nodding at my gloved hands.

"Freezing." I lie, attempting to curl my hand into a fist, but the stiff gold leaves my fingers bending like claws. "Will I be seeing you at the next exhibition?"

"One thing was agreeing with your first stunt, but this..." she trails off, her brows knitting together to form a V-shaped worry line.

"Is it the mausoleum you aren't a fan of?" I say with a smile.

"Those places give me the creeps," she says, shuddering, her movements exaggerated.

"That's the whole point," I add. "Art is supposed to make you feel something."

"If I wanted to puke, I would just get myself food poisoning," she argues, but her features soften. "Anyway, what can I get for you?"

"Get me the lasagna again," I reply, the discordance of the two women piercing my ears.

While she's busy in the kitchen, I catch a glimpse of someone outside the bar. I barely have to turn my head to realise who he is—nor do I have much time to let the dread wash over me.

The one-eyed man enters through the swinging door and a gush of cool air makes the flyers placed in front of me flutter slightly. They tremble, pinched to the clip in their holder. *Trapped.*

He takes a seat right next to me, the worn leather complaining under his weight.

His gaze is fixed on the liquor bottles behind the bar as he curls his hands in front of him on the counter.

Is he mocking me?

My heart is beating out of my chest, my throat suddenly parched. As I glance out at the street, the shadowy figures are wavering, but their eyes have grown more piercing. They aren't looking at me.

They're looking at him.

"Here you go," the bartender chirps, extending her words melodically.

She doesn't notice the man, not even a hint of recognition.

It's like he isn't even here.

My hand trembles so violently beneath the glove, that my fork clinks against the porcelain. I eat awkwardly with my good hand, shoving down the steaming hot pasta. I burn my tongue, but I keep going until the plate is empty.

The bartender frowns at me.

"Someone's in a rush," she says.

The women have finally handed over the microphone to a young guy, whose vocal chords ring out like smooth ripples on the surface of a calm lake.

When the one-eyed man turns to face me, the neon sign above the bar flickers irregularly, strangely slowly like a weakening pulse.

"You can't keep hiding, you know," he says flatly. "It always catches up with you in the end." I stutter something incoherent in a muffled voice, nearly replying, until I notice the bartender is staring at me. I turn towards her, but the man continues. "Your work will consume you," he says. "You are still becoming—" but the bartender's voice overlaps his.

"Are you okay?" she asks, her golden hair tied in a bun at the nape of her neck.

Perhaps gold should be kept in strands on a pretty blonde, rather than be herded into obedience by the laws of flesh.

"Times are changing," I reply cryptically. "You have to keep up with it if you want to succeed."

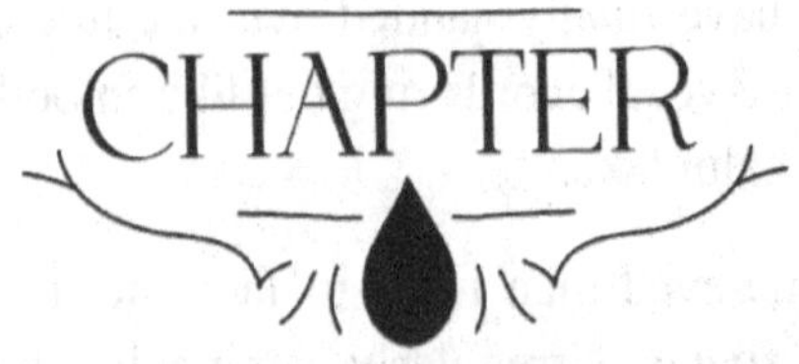

16: DEATH REIMAGINED

The following Wednesday I'm pacing my empty studio with a hollow sensation in my chest. The truck has just picked up my artwork and as it slips further away—heading for the mausoleum—the dark figures seem to multiply in their absence. They are twisting their faces at me, as though trying to cry out and taunt me. I narrow my eyes at them, and they briefly step back again.

My manager insists I wear a suit for the occasion, a request I begrudgingly agreed to. It feels suffocating. *Rigid.* I pull my tie loose and discard it before a familiar series of honks reverberate from the street below. I grab my keys and wallet, and meet my driver on the sidewalk.

He opens the back door for me, and I slide in. A young guy skates past my window as we set off towards the exhibition.

I've been wearing gloves ever since the gold spread further, but the sudden absence of movement in it is almost more disturbing to me than the actual, parasite-like behaviour.

I want it to spread, I think, before shaking off the intrusive thought.

Tombstones appear in a neatly fenced graveyard along the roadside. My driver pulls into the courtyard of the *Cimitero Monumentale* where the mausoleum is located. I traverse the steps to the main building as the press flashes their cameras in my direction. Two guards are awaiting the signal to let in the crowd, and my manager is right by the entrance to greet me.

"*Tutto bene*," he chirps. "This will be excellent, just excellent. Come with me and I will introduce you to Rafael."

Inside, the dark floor and the iconic white and brown horizontal stripes that line the towering walls create a grandiose atmosphere.

We stride through the foyer, into the first chamber. In the centre, a large stone coffin is surrounded by a dozen of Rafael's pastel creations. Long strips of light spill in, casting skeletal shadows in their wake.

"There are... so many?" I blurt out, right before I lay eyes on him.

"Ah, my clients meet at last," my manager exclaims. "Rafael, this is Bart."

I mechanically extend my good hand, and Rafael grabs it with both of his in an eager, light-hearted gesture. His dark, curly hair is cropped just above the ears, and his tie matches the skeletons with its bubbly shades of baby blue.

"Such a pleasure," Rafael says, seeming genuine.

"Let me give you the grand tour before we let in the public," my manager says. "Come along, come along."

Down the hallway, Rafael's skeletons are seamlessly blending in with my models. Some skeletons are posing as mirror images of the models in front of them, while others appear to be caught mid-step in a dance, their boney fingers entwined with each other.

As we near the two crypts where each of my framed pieces are exhibited, the light fades until it is nearly pitch dark. A few candles flicker their orange glow to illuminate the entrance to each burial chamber, but they barely flicker in the stagnant air.

A cool, damp scent emanates from within, and I narrow my eyes before stepping inside. Rafael and my manager enter the room cautiously, keeping their distance.

The glow from the vitrine casts a ring of light on the uneven stone floor. My pulse quickens, thudding in my ears and the looming shadows pull back to allow me to study the piece. Just like at the gallery, speakers are pulsating with a deep bass rhythm, bringing the room to life. It looks perfect—vibrant colours ignoring the passing of time. It'll stay like this forever.

I retreat to the corridor before entering the opposite chamber.

J-Way's chamber.

Just before I touch the handle of the ancient door, I decide to let Rafael step in ahead of me. I hold the door open, as I witness their first encounter.

His breath catches at the sight of the gold, his fingers twitching by his sides. I like knowing that he is impressed, awestruck even—but something doesn't feel quite right. The room is hot, much unlike the first chamber. As I join him inside, the gold moves under my skin, tracing across my shoulder and onto my chest. I feel ensnared. Like the noose is tightening to an inescapable degree.

We both pull back, exiting in haste without a word.

"You really did something with that," Rafael admits, his cheeks flushing from the heat. "But you might want to turn down the temperature. That was a bit... extreme."

I simply nod, and *our* manager escorts us back to the front entrance to greet the guests. The first group is fascinated, even sharing muffled laughter as they circle the first part of the exhibition. But when they return from the chambers, their expressions are flat and horrified—*my art is superior in every way.*

A single woman lingers outside J-Way's chamber, with lips parted as though words were caught in her throat. Her arms are straight along her sides, and her gaze is fixed on something invisible ahead.

Not long after, I spot Rafael deep in conversation with my old art teacher, Mr. Del Vago. The old man listens intently to Rafael's words, nodding between every other sentence. I circle closer, but their conversation is barely audible. I don't know what I want to do. I don't know if I want to do anything at all—until I hear Rafael's voice.

"Speaking of the devil!" he says cheerfully. "Bart, I believe this is your former teacher! Truly a man with an eye for detail."

I half-turn, and Mr. Del Vago looks me dead in the eye.

The two men shake hands before parting ways. The crowd is ebbing and flowing around us, moving like the sea. Mr. Del Vago's suit is identical to the ones he used to wear during classes. Under the pressure of his scrutinising glare, I am diminished to a boy with a pencil in my hand. I could drown in his presence, my insides gasping for air.

He doesn't speak. He simply clenches his jaw, before adjusting his tie. A few, suffocating moments pass before he nods towards the hallway leading to the chambers, shakes his head—*and leaves*.

...

Around noon, someone taps me on the shoulder. I'm mildly disoriented from the constant influx of guests, so at first I barely notice. They tap me again, almost apologetically.

When I turn, the bartender is smiling crookedly at me, before pressing her lips together. She's standing right in front of one of the tall windows, the light playing with her golden hair.

"Hi Bart," she says shyly.

The tension in my shoulders subsides and I mirror her smile. It's good to see her. I immediately feel more anchored in the moment.

"You never told me your name," I say, tilting my head slightly.

Someone interrupts us, asking for my autograph. I sign it with half an eye before sending them a tight smile.

"Giulia," she replies. "I never thought you'd ask."

"I never thought you'd come," I say. Scanning the room, her gaze doesn't linger on Rafael's skeletons, nor on the stone casket. Instead, her eyes meet mine once more. "Did you see my new artwork yet?" I ask, challenging her, well knowing she hasn't.

"God, no—" she says, her eyes widening. "I just thought I'd drop by, as a friend, or—"

"...as a fan?" I chuckle. "Let me show you," I add, already two steps in the direction of the corridor before realising she isn't following me.

Her shoulders raise and her body stiffens, so despite myself, I turn to her, hand extended.

"You can close your eyes if it's too much," I tease.

She looks at me for a moment before her nimble fingers slide across the palm of my ungloved hand. I squeeze it slightly as I place the other hand in my pocket to avoid questions.

Together, we walk through the corridor, one, slow step at a time. With her along, every stride feels like a dance, her movements effortless and curious. We halt for a moment by the edge of the darkness as a group of people exits the left chamber, their faces cast in shadow.

I hold my ground when the group passes, but Giulia grabs my arm as she steps aside, pulling herself closer to me. The top of her head grazes my chin and the scent of her hair sends ripples of heat through me.

My closest model shifts her weight, goosebumps visible on the surface of her exposed skin. I clear my throat.

Giulia steps back, blushing, but we quickly continue towards J-Way's chamber without a word.

Pulling the door open with a long, moaning creak, she steps inside. I follow her, letting the door slide shut behind us.

Thud, thud, the speakers tremble.

Giulia steps around the frame, her eyes searching every detail. She pauses right in front of the vitrine, her back facing me.

"Bart," she whispers as though not to wake the dead. "It's like... he is still here."

My chest tightens at her words, my breaths growing shallow as I feel the golden veins take further hold of me.

There is no pain, only bliss—until I see the goddess stretching her fingers on the dehydrated skin.

"I better get going," she says immediately. "My shift begins at five and I need to drop by my apartment and—"

"It's no problem," I interrupt, swallowing the lump in my throat.

She places a brief hand on my arm before rushing out of the chamber, leaving me behind.

17: CORUSCATING SPLENDOUR

Right in front of my eyes, the golden moon on J-Way's skin begins to glow. As I stare at the orb, it slowly fades to red, and I recoil at the sudden flush of heat emanating from the case. It is smouldering—reaching a fever pitch before the moon begins to melt. Drops of crimson stream down the fleshy canvas, the golden clouds stirring in coruscating splendour.

The dark figures reappear suddenly, glitching into existence. Their long nails dig into the rotten flesh on their faces and rip gashes through which they begin to scream.

SUCH A SHAME, SUCH A SHAME.

Their voices grow louder as the skin begins to droop, their hissing forming an earsplitting choir.

SHAME, SHAME.

I reach out, fumbling in the darkness as the light in the case goes out.

"No!" I shriek. "No!"

I can hear footsteps approaching from the stone corridor, and within seconds, my manager is by my side.

The candlelight from the hallway casts a weak glow on the artwork.

It is as pristine as ever.

"What happened?" my manager exclaims, pulling me out of the dark chamber by the wrist. "We're closing the exhibition for today, the press is awaiting your exit. Make it grand."

Heat continues to seep through the open door to the chamber, sending rippling waves through the air. As the models gather their belongings and head for the exit, only the skeletons remain in the dim corridor. I cast a quick glance down the hall before grabbing the collar of my cruel, white shirt.

My manager frowns at me, lifting a single eyebrow.

Instead of speaking, I unbutton my shirt and expose my golden chest, gritting my teeth.

"*Mamma mia*," he whispers, placing a hand on his temple. He doesn't glance twice at my chest, as though there's nothing to see. "Bart, button your shirt. Do you have a fever? We will get you to the hospital. But first, the press awaits us."

...

The front hall is desolate, our dress shoes clicking against the linoleum floor. My manager steps ahead of me to open the double doors wide, and I stride down the steps with a rhythmic flow as the journalists snap the latest front news photographs. Rafael is already gesticulating with wide, exaggerated movements as he tells the tale of his oath to success.

At the foot of the stone steps, the crowd gathers in a half circle, encircling us with their hawk-like stares as I join his side. My skin is clammy and burning hot.

"Bart, tell us about your greatest inspiration," one says eagerly.

"How does it feel to—" another tries, but Rafael interrupts.

"This collaboration has been a turning point in our careers," he says in a loud and clear voice, placing a tight arm around me.

I try to keep a straight face, but I grunt as my body is painfully sore. He pulls away at the sound, bemused.

I turn to face the first journalist, poised with determination to outshine Rafael despite my discomfort.

"This has surely been a... transformative experience," I begin, "...a manifestation of a new era, where the end is but another beginning."

"Where are you looking to take this opportunity next?" someone asks, the wind tugging at her hair.

"Why ruin the fun by telling you?"

I smirk before pushing my way through to the sidewalk where my driver awaits me. The crowd continues to shout their questions at me, but I shut them out. Rafael's voice reverberates against the façade.

Sure, embarrass yourself.

When I enter the car, the same hollow feeling from this morning builds inside of me as the mausoleum disappears behind a corner. I cannot be separated from my art, and yet—its very presence consumes me.

My foot taps the floor as my leg bounces up and down. When we reach my street, I hurry up to change out of the shirt. What should have taken a minute seems to have been stretched into an hour, because when I return to the street, the sun has already set. I furrow my brows at the distorted sense of time, shrugging it off. My body feels strangely numb.

Giulia greets me with a shy smile, apologising yet again for her sudden departure earlier.

I wave it off with my gloved hand, keeping the other on my restless knee below the table.

"You made my day," I admit.

"What's with the gloves, anyway," she asks, diverting the attention from herself, but another patron waves for her to bring another pair of pints to their table.

While she fills the glasses, she tilts her head, focusing. I observe her every movement, the way she always purses her lips whenever someone addresses her. The way her hair catches the light.

She serves the guests before returning to her usual position, and lowers her voice as she leans across the counter with an elbow on the sticky surface.

“Today changed something in me,” she says thoughtfully. "It’s like you said, art is supposed to evoke feelings.”

“I thought it disturbed you?” I ask quizzically.

“It did, but—” she says, drawing back just enough to look straight at me, her eyes searching mine. “It made me realise just how stuck I am. I should be moving on with my life, not tend to the same bar for eternity.” I let out a slight sigh, a crooked smile forming on my lips. My lungs are burning, and I suddenly feel cold. “And staying here...” she adds, her voice barely audible above the music. “I’m not allowed to engage with my customers like this, it’s against the code of conduct.”

“Then where do you expect me to go and get my daily, mediocre pasta?” I tease, surprising even myself.

“I cook quite well,” she replies.

She cooks quite well?

“Where would you go, then?”

She pauses, visibly thinking.

“Well, I thought—” she begins, before shaking her head.

“No, what did you think?” I pry.

"I sort of always dreamed about tattooing myself," she says. "Like, going to the school in Rome to learn. Or maybe find a... local apprenticeship. Something like that, but—"

"But what?"

"But then I'd probably have the same problem as here," she says without further explanation, blushing in a shade of dusty rose.

The way her cheeks flush makes her eyes stand out.

She serves one more customer, then takes her time wiping a few tables. She smiles at me briefly, while counting the cash in the register. It seems a bit early for that, but I don't comment.

"Will you still be here in let's say... twenty?"

"Sure," I reply. "Sure."

She's gone much longer than her usual breaks, and in her absence, my void seems to grow. My body begins to ache as though I've been stripped of something crucial. My hand feels sore, and my shoulder feels bruised.

When she returns, though, she's wearing the same outfit as she did at the exhibition—and her lips are painted ruby red. Any remaining discomfort in my body is replaced by a sudden, unusual desire.

"I just quit," she says enigmatically, sliding her band along the counter as she comes to take a seat next to me. "You better be worth it," she adds, her eyes gleaming in the neon light.

"You did that for me?" My lips part as though to say something further, but she quickly places a hand on mine.

"Your selfishness is rubbing off on me," she chuckles. "I did this for myself." With those words, she grabs her coat, and we step out onto the sidewalk. "You could show me the studio?" she suggests. "*Prep* me for my new aspiration."

"Sure, I—" I say, but before I can say *maybe another day*, she's crossing the road.

I have a strange knot in my stomach, one I can't quite place.

The moment we enter the studio, Giulia takes my hand and pulls me towards her, guiding my hand to her side—but in the same motion, her eyes grow alarmed and her brows furrow. She pulls away from me wordlessly, her eyes tracing my arm all the way down to our hands.

They are covered in sticky, dried blood.

In the absence of noise, my breaths seem louder.

Then she breaks the silence.

"Did you punch the mirror?" Giulia asks quietly, looking doe-eyed between my hands and the cracks in the mirror.

"What?"

The concern in her eyes is slowly replaced by something closer to fear, her pupils dilating.

"You punched the mirror?"

I look at the wall only to see fragments of reality reflected back at us, the floor scattered with splinters.

The bruised knuckles on my left hand grow warm as Giulia lets go of me. She begins shaking her head slowly—an involuntary movement of denial—before she snaps back to her senses, stepping backwards.

She disappears down the stairs, out of the building.

Out of my life.

EPILOGUE

Around 9am, I wake with a tingling sensation in my golden left hand. When the art arrived last night as planned, I left them covered for the sake of my own sanity, but now the hand seems to twitch at the very thought.

Entering the studio in my underwear, the strange heat emanating from J-Way's case seems fainter now—yet it still persists. The shattered mirrors portray the room at peculiar angles, and for a moment, I see a partial reflection of Giulia's face as though she was still here. As though part of her still wanted to stay.

I raise my golden hand and pull the drape off the artwork. The surface of the vitrine reflects a translucent depiction of my transformed self. Slightly warped by the bright overhead light, almost mingling with the tattoo on J-Way's skin.

Have we become as one, brother? I think, as the waves around the goddess stir, clashing against her golden silhouette. As I stare at it, an alluring song of sirens drifts towards me. Every note echoes in my skull. With each splash of the waves, my golden skin extends further. I embrace it, *breathe into it*, as though pushing my life beyond the boundaries of man.

Man, I think. *No, that will no longer suffice.*

A hard crack forms in the glass, and the stench of rotten flesh betrays his presence.

"You aren't wrong," the familiar, distinctly cool voice says. I stare, unblinking, as the gold seeps into my veins. The one-eyed man sucks his teeth, witnessing my collapse without flinching. He towers rigidly above me, his hat casting a shadow across his brow as my body contorts from deprivation. *Oxygen. Life.* The edges of my vision pulsate into a tightening vignette as his final words strip me like flesh from bone. "*But now you're just another body ready for display.*"

ABOUT THE AUTHOR

The Danish author Line Langager (b. 1998) debuted as a writer in 2024 with the surreal and tender short story 'The Milk Carton' and the children's book 'Our Friend Kattan'. Her tales shed light on human behavior and the magic of the ordinary with a fluent, poetic language and captivating scenes. Several of her works have been published in literary magazines or anthologies. She particularly enjoys the freedom of magical realism and dystopian fiction, since her chronic illness, Myalgic Encephalomyelitis, has left her bed-bound.

Find her online @author.line.langager on Instagram and Threads!

www.ingramcontent.com/pod-product-compliance
Lightning Source LLC
LaVergne TN
LVHW030912080826
845145LV00010B/2870